CW01373873

HUEYS OVER KHE SANH

HUEYS OVER KHE SANH

Missions with VMO-6

PETER GREENE

CASEMATE
Pennsylvania & Yorkshire

Published in the United States of America and Great Britain in 2024 by
CASEMATE PUBLISHERS
1950 Lawrence Road, Havertown, PA 19083, USA
and
47 Church Street, Barnsley, S70 2AS, UK

Copyright © 2024 Peter Greene

Hardcover Edition: 978-1-63624-445-7
Digital Edition: 978-1-63624-446-4

A CIP record for this book is available from the British Library

All rights reserved. No part of this book may be reproduced or transmitted in any form or by any means, electronic or mechanical including photocopying, recording or by any information storage and retrieval system, without permission from the publisher in writing.

Printed and bound in CPI Group (UK) Ltd, Croydon, CR0 4YY
Typeset in India by DiTech Publishing Services

For a complete list of Casemate titles, please contact:

CASEMATE PUBLISHERS (US)
Telephone (610) 853-9131
Fax (610) 853-9146
Email: casemate@casematepublishers.com
www.casematepublishers.com

CASEMATE PUBLISHERS (UK)
Telephone (0)1226 734350
Email: casemate@casemateuk.com
www.casemateuk.com

All images from author's collection.

Contents

Preface		vii
1	My Background	1
2	Enlistment and USMC Boot Camp	7
3	Off to War	15
4	Culture Shock	21
5	A Brief History of VMO-6	31
6	Time to Start Flying	35
7	Land Shark	51
8	Support for SOG	57
9	The Hill Battles at Khe Sanh	69
10	CH-46 Downed	73
11	A Hard Day's Night	83
12	Couldn't Find the Bullet Hole	91
13	Night Standby	95
14	Last Missions from Ky Ha	99
15	The Move to Phu Bai	107
16	Quang Tri Air Base	111
17	Young Vietnamese Girl	117
18	Technical Problems	119
19	The Sniffer	127
20	Mortar Attack	129
21	Con Thien Overrun	135
22	Enemy in the Open	143
23	No Joy	147
24	SOG Team in Trouble	151

25	Gio Linh Resupply	157
26	Leaving Vietnam	165
27	Back Home in the States	171
28	Reunions and Reflections	177

Citations   182

Preface

In January 1966, like millions of young men graduating from high school, we were facing a difficult fate, the Vietnam War and the draft. With rare exception, unless you were enrolled in college as a full-time student or had already started a family or were classified as "4-F," most likely you were going into the US military. I decided to enlist in the Marine Corps, and to this day I am proud of that fact and that I serviced in Marine Aviation and VMO-6 for 13 months in Vietnam. I am proud of the service I performed, and the fact that I have been able to write about my experiences I had with a USMC helicopter gunship squadron, VMO-6.

I believe that I can speak for the other crew chiefs and squadron mates who shared the role of the gunner, and hope that I am not stepping on anyone's toes; I am writing this book about my own experiences and events that I have had and have seen during my tour. I know that each and every one of the pilots and other crew chiefs has had their own unique experiences, events, and "shit sandwiches" which only they can recount in detail. Hopefully, the day will come when I can get this published, and no doubt some of the other guys, or crew chiefs, will remember and recognize some of these missions as they could have been the "lead" or the "chase" bird on any given day.

With rare exceptions, I do not remember who the pilot or crew might have been on a given day. But they will all agree that every day each of us had numerous missions, and rarely did we return to base without needing to rearm the birds. I hope that after more than 50 years I can accurately describe some of the events I witnessed and was involved with during my tour; though they took place over a half-century ago, many seem like yesterday, permanently planted in my head. I can only wish that I had finished this several months ago, as I would have liked to have acknowledged and complimented all three of our commanding officers, Lieutenant Colonels Maloney, Nelson, and White, before time took them away.

CHAPTER I

My Background

I was born in Houlton, Maine in 1945. My father, Arthur F. Greene, was a soldier stationed there at the US Army base on the US/Canadian border at the end of World War II; it was there that he met and married my mother, Barbara Hare, who lived nearby at Monticello, Maine. Other than farming potatoes or working in the woods, there was not a lot of opportunity for a young family in northern Maine. Soon after the war, while I was just a toddler my mother and father moved to the northern Kentucky area across the Ohio river from Cincinnati, where my father found work. They settled in Dayton, KY on the other side of the river; this is where I grew up and lived until Vietnam called. I was the oldest of eight children; the first six of us were boys. My parents divorced after the first four boys when I was about seven years old, and my mother remarried a year later to my stepfather, John Torrey. They had four more children and they are my stepbrothers and sisters. My full brothers are Richard, Timothy, and Kim Greene; my stepfamily is John, Mark, Cathi and Melissa Torrey.

I attended a couple of area schools as a youngster, then soon after my mother remarried my stepfather John, we converted to the Catholic religion, and I attended St. Bernard's middle school in the sixth, seventh, and eighth grades. I am still a Catholic to this day. Afterward, I attended and graduated from Dayton High School in 1963. Coming from a large family, my brother Richard and I started working after middle school, stocking shelves at local grocery stores to help support the family. After high school, my first real job was working for Wiedemann Brewery in Newport, KY; I worked in the office of the shipping department. I was only an average student in high school, but my favorite subject was accounting, and after I started working at Wiedemann I enrolled in accounting classes at the University of Cincinnati, attending late afternoon and evening classes. My desire was to get an associate degree and then go on to become a CPA.

During high school and afterward, I started chumming around with one of my best friends to this day, Tom Arens. Tom attended Newport Catholic High School; he then introduced me to some of his friends who went to school there. Before long we had formed a bond and started hanging out together all the time, and we called ourselves the TRG (Thunder Road Gang): Bill Vonderhaar, Bill Twehues, Rick Volmer, Roy Vories, Mike Faeth, Tom, and myself. After a while, several more of their friends joined us: John Becker, Steve Saner, and Ken Heilburg. There was nothing bad, mischievous, or arrogant about us; we were just cool, and none of us got in trouble with the law (though I was lucky several times with the way I drove my car). Every time I hear the Beach Boys song, "I Get Around," with the lyric "the bad guys know us, and they leave us alone," I think of TRG. Then there were the girls that we used to hang out with, Darlene, Judy, Sue, Barbara, Kathy, and others; after a while, they started calling themselves the "TRG-ettes." Those were certainly very fond memories for me.

Getting back to my first real job at Wiedemann, I really liked working there for several reasons; it was a great place to work, the company paid for my college tuition at UC, if I maintained a "C" average, which I managed to do, and lastly, free beer. Even though I was only 18, and the drinking age in Kentucky was 21, nobody ever said anything. Occasionally I would have ice-cold beer; every office had a refrigerator full of beer. And for the workforce out in the bottling plant and elsewhere there was the "Tap Room." It was staffed with full-time bartenders, and each employee got a five-minute beer break every couple of hours. Kentucky was mostly hot and humid in the summer, even more so for those working in the bottling plant area; everything was on the up and up, if the employees behaved themselves and did not get intoxicated. The other cool thing for me was on Friday and Saturday nights before the TRG headed out looking for girls, I would bring the guys down to the Tap

Room for a couple of beers; nobody ever objected. In addition, during my second summer at Wiedemann after work on Fridays, I would often buy two-quarter barrels of beer for the beach parties that we would throw on the weekends on the banks of the Ohio River. I would have bought a half-barrel, but I couldn't lift one into the trunk of my car. Another plus: I was buying the beer at wholesale prices.

Fortunately, I was very lucky; we never got into trouble with the law, but still, being underage, I could have got not only myself but Wiedemann in big trouble. Finally, I came to my senses and stopped buying beer at my place of employment. Back in those days we never had any trouble buying a case of beer at the local stores and bars anyway; that's just the way it was back in the '60s. I never fully realized it while goofing off in those days, and before Vietnam became the big issue, but the area we frequented in and around Newport, Kentucky was nationally known as "Sin City USA." Apparently, there was a lot of organized crime in Newport run by the local Mafia, but we—or I—just didn't realize it.

There were a couple of times while out with the guys having "a beer or two" when John Becker and I would race our cars, his '54 Chevy and my '55 Ford, and it is truly a wonder that I am still alive today, because of my stupidity. The one event that I will never forget was when somebody dared us to race. I had Rick Volmer with me, John had someone else with him. The road coming from Ft. Thomas into Newport was somewhat downhill and at the bottom it turned, first right then left. Both cars were nose to nose with neither one of us willing to give up the race with trouble just ahead. At the first turn to the right, I felt the passenger side wheels start to lift. What stupidity! Thank God, we both hit the brakes and avoided rolling the cars over. For sure, I certainly was no saint in my younger days, but sometimes idiocy cannot be ruled out when you're young and you've consumed several beers and feel like you can do anything.

★★★

In November 1963, President John F. Kennedy was assassinated and suddenly the world we knew was beginning to change. Most of us had never even heard of Vietnam, but shortly after Kennedy's death, the reality of the coming war and the draft became the paramount issue that held everyone's attention, especially young guys right out of high school.

During that time, and back to our "Thunder Road Gang" days, there would always be several of us on weekends out riding around, looking for girls and having fun. But one thing that I will always remember is Bill Vonderhaar's reaction whenever we would drive by a billboard advertising the Marine Corps. He had already developed the "esprit de corps," and his goal even then was the USMC, and becoming a Marine officer. I believe he was the first of us to know what he wanted in life; he was soon to be leaving for the University of Kentucky to get his degree and the first step toward getting his commission.

With Vietnam in the picture, it was obvious that I was not going to be able to stay in school, as you had to carry at least 15 credit hours to be considered full-time and thus defer the draft. During my second year at Cincinnati, I started advanced accounting and added business administration and was hoping to get close to an associate degree, then later become a certified public accountant; but that was not going to happen. I did not want to be drafted and decided to enlist in the USMC. My friend John Becker, likewise, decided on the Marine Corps; John and I had become more excited about joining the USMC, so we decided that we would enlist together on the "buddy system." I knew that John was mechanically inclined, was very good at working on an automobile, and that he did all the repairs on his Chevrolet. As for me, I really didn't have any skills.

I am proud of the fact that all five of my brothers and I served in the US military. My brother Richard (Dick) was the first to enlist, into the US navy; Tim enlisted in the Marines immediately after I rotated home and was sent to Nam, stationed at Da Nang. Kim joined the Marines a year and a half after Tim, and he became a crew chief on the Harrier jet. John enlisted for two tours in the navy and served aboard an aircraft carrier, while Mark opted for the US Air Force and was stationed in Alaska.

And I would add that my wife Kathy and I had two daughters, Amanda and Pamela. Pamela decided to enlist into the Marine Corps immediately after high school (I swear I had nothing to do with it) and today she is Lieutenant Colonel Pamela Unger and is the financial comptroller at Camp Lejeune, NC. A year after enlisting, Pam married another Marine; both were in the enlisted ranks at the time but went on to become officers. Pam's husband Mark (Major Mark Unger, USMC ret) was initially a CH-46 helicopter pilot, then a V-22 Osprey pilot, and a V-22 instructor when he retired. And another family member I am proud to acknowledge, and who also enlisted in the USMC: Amanda's daughter, and my granddaughter, Elizabeth (Libby) Gallant. However, Libby injured her hip in boot camp and then after two years of attempted rehabilitation was medically discharged; during that time Libby met and married another Marine, her husband Jorge Hernandez, while they were stationed in Okinawa.

In these last paragraphs, it sounds like I am bragging about all the Marines in my immediate family, and I suppose that I am, but I can assure you I had absolutely nothing to do with any of them enlisting into the USMC. It was entirely their choice. My only explanation is that they were all probably trying to outdo the "old jarhead" of the family, and probably they have.

CHAPTER 2

Enlistment and USMC Boot Camp

In January 1966 I was working at Wiedemann Brewery and attending night classes at the University of Cincinnati. I knew that the draft was catching up with me; I was hoping to finish the semester and get the credits, but I did not want to get drafted into the army. So John and I visited the USMC recruiting station, and we explained our thoughts to the recruiter. It was then that the recruiter suggested that he could make that happen, if we opted for Marine Aviation. I'm sure neither of us had much of an idea exactly what Marine Aviation was. But it made sense, so both John and I were sworn in January, and scheduled to start boot camp in early March '66. And I received my credits for the semester.

After the semester ended, I got a letter from my mother's grandparents in Maine (Granny and Papa Porter). They were in their eighties and concerned about me going into the Marine Corps and Vietnam. Our fondest childhood memories are when the family would pile into the car and drive non-stop to Maine for a week or so to visit my mother's family in Monticello. My brothers Dick, Tim and I were middle-school age during those summer trips, and we loved to play in Papa's barn where he made three swings for us. We would bring in and stack the firewood that he had delivered, then he gave us each a dollar. Several during our visit he would make pancakes for breakfast on their wood stove' I'll always remember him half laughing and half exasperated, trying to keep up with three hungry mouths to feed. He used to call Gram "the old woman" when she wasn't around, and we weren't allowed to go in her parlor because we'd get it dirty. Those were very happy days. I'll never forget at the end of one of those trips, we had loaded up the car, we were leaving and heading back to KY, and there was Papa standing by the car with tears running down his cheeks. Two weeks before heading off for boot camp I flew to Maine to visit my grandparents and Aunt Chavala again. I'm so glad I did, as Papa passed away a year and half later while I was in Nam.

March arrived and there were seven of us Marine recruits leaving for boot camp. Just before we flew out of Cincinnati Airport (which is in Covington, KY), late that afternoon for that first night and the start of boot camp, the recruiter handed me a very large manila envelope. For whatever reason they picked yours truly to carry the records and orders for all seven of us. I remember the last thing the recruiter said to me that afternoon before we boarded the plane for San Diego: "DO NOT let this package out of your sight, there will be a Marine there to pick you guys up."

When our flight departed Cincinnati Airport, we first flew to Chicago, and then on to San Diego. I really didn't notice at the time, but at O'Hare, a bunch of guys our age also boarded the flight. When the plane landed in San Diego at about 11pm, and as we entered the terminal, there were Marines and navy everywhere, coming and going. After a few minutes, I was getting nervous about carrying all the paperwork for the seven of us and I started asking, "Are you here to pick us up?" Finally, I asked the right Marine, and he immediately punched me in the stomach, knocking the wind out of me. I was on the terminal floor gasping for air, trying to get my breath back, with this Marine standing over me and screaming, "Don't you ever call me a fucking ewe again, you fucking scumbag, it that clear?" I will never forget it. As it turned out, with the other guys on the flight out of Chicago, there were 85 of us: all recruits on the same plane, and it turned out to be our platoon at boot camp, Platoon #178.

There is no need to explain anything about USMC boot camp; it was notoriously tough. Ask any Marine and they'll tell you that once was enough. I know of no one who wants to do it again. But times have certainly changed since the six Marine recruits who died at Parris Island. For decades now it's been illegal for drill instructors (DIs) to physically hit anyone, but that was not the case in the 1960s. I found that out at the airport, but there were others in the platoon who later would learn it for themselves.

That first night at boot camp seemed unreal. In a flash, we were on the bus getting screamed at by three drill instructors, then after a very short ride and before we knew it, we were all standing on those famous yellow footprints that every Marine remembers.

It was almost midnight when we arrived at USMC Recruit Depot, and if you can believe, in the next four hours, our heads had been shaved bald, we were all stripped down naked, shipped all our clothes home, and all 85 of us were in the shower room for perhaps 10 minutes, all the while with DIs screaming at us.

Standing in a line buck naked, we were issued a footlocker, side-stepping in a line holding the footlockers while other Marines were screaming at each one of us, what size shirt, waist and leg size, what size boot, every little thing that we would need to get started. About three hours later, marching in the dark, we arrived at our new home, the Quonset huts. They lined us up and assigned us to the Quonset huts, which had about 10 bunk beds, five on each side. There were sheets, a pillow, and a blanket on each bunk, and in very short order the DIs showed us how to correctly make our beds. Finally, it was time to hit the rack; however, it was perhaps 15 minutes after they yelled "lights out" when suddenly, at exactly 4:30am, reveille sounded and the DIs came busting through the doors screaming at us: "OUTSIDE, OUT FUCKING SIDE, every one of you fucking swinging dicks outside in formation in five minutes." Welcome to the Marine Corps!

It was unbelievable how fast they ran us through that procedure. I won't bore you any further with other stuff that we went through, but USMC boot camp is everything that you have heard about. And once was enough.

One thing that I can tell you about boot camp, at least in Platoon #178: the word "fuck" was very much part of the DI boot camp vocabulary. It was used numerous times in every sentence spoken by the DI's. I can't tell you how many times we heard, "You are going to be lean, mean, foul mouth fucking Marines, IF and WHEN you fucking make it out of here." However, in defense of the USMC, I will add here that contrary to the boot camp environment and Platoon #178's younger and junior drill instructors, with their colorful and descriptive language, that was not necessarily the case afterward. Turning boys and young men into Marines in just three months had its challenges; in fact, it was very remarkable. Most of us (but not all) somewhat cleaned up our everyday language when we graduated from boot camp and into the regular Marine Corps, and then re-entered normal society.

I'll never forget how in such a short period of time, in three months, those DIs transformed us from "a fucking herd of cattle" into a seasoned platoon as we were getting close to graduation. There were dozens of platoons in various stages of training in boot camp, and several times while we were marching, or trying to march as a Marine platoon, the lead drill instructor would happen to notice a seasoned platoon heading in our direction, a platoon that was getting close to graduation: "You fucking bunch of shitbirds, get the fuck off the fucking street, bow your fucking heads; here comes some real fucking Marines."

It certainly was impressive watching them march by, the whole platoon of 85–90 seasoned recruits soon to graduate from boot camp; all you could hear was just one heel hitting the deck as they marched by in perfect unison. Their utility uniforms and soft covers (hats) were starched and pressed; they were totally squared away. They looked every bit of the word "sharp," and they knew it. I couldn't wait for my turn to be just like them.

The platoon was divided into four squads. John and I ended up in different squads, different Quonset huts, and really didn't get to see each other very much; but it didn't matter, there was absolutely no time for socializing anyway, we were always on the run and on the go. Even at "chow" at the mess hall, the whole platoon was in and out in about 20 minutes; then it was off for the next class or event. But I think I can speak for most recruits who went through Marine boot camp when I say our biggest fear was getting hurt, either on the obstacle course, in hand-to-hand combat, or any number of ways while in training; if you got hurt or injured to the point that you could not immediately continue, they would send you to "Casualty Platoon" to recover, and then you would have to start boot camp all over in a new platoon.

Midway through boot camp, we were bussed up to Camp Pendleton to train on the rifle range. We were there for two weeks learning to shoot the M-1 rifle, and the Marine Corps prides itself on producing excellent riflemen. The first week at the range was "snapping in"; using the rifle sling and twisting it around your arm and elbow to hold the rifle steady. The first couple of days of "snapping in" were painful until you got used to it. In the second week, we started live firing at 200, 300, and 500 yards. However, at midweek, there was too much wind for "live" fire, so they took us on another of those many long runs. Later that afternoon, they split us up to do various work details in and around the administration building, and John and I happened to be in the same group cleaning and polishing the floors inside the building. There happened to be a radio playing inside one of the offices; it was the first time any of us had heard a radio and any music since before the start of boot camp. After a few minutes, the Beach Boys' new song, "Sloop John B," started playing. As we listened to the lyrics, "this is the worst trip I've ever been on," and "let me go home," those words were so coincidental, and fitting to our situation, we immediately both realized that it was a perfect fit for John B. Becker. He would be known as "Sloop John B" for the rest of his days.

We didn't realize it back then, but when John and I enlisted in the USMC in January, to start boot camp in March, Steve Saner had received his draft notice. The day he reported to the draft board was the first time that the USMC had resorted to the draft for recruits. When Steve reported, there was a Marine recruiter there also, looking for "a few good men." Steve also decided to enlist in the USMC. Little did we know, but Steve had already been sworn in and had started boot camp two months earlier than John and me.

As it turned out, we were all at USMC Recruit Training Depot in San Diego at the same time but didn't know it. Steve was in the final phases of boot camp when John and I had just started, and more than likely, he was in one of those seasoned platoons getting ready to graduate that we saw that day when our DI told us to get off the fucking street and watch the real Marines march by. Steve was given a 0311 MOS (Infantry). After boot camp and infantry training, he was given leave and then immediately ordered on to "WEST-PAC": Vietnam. He would start his 13-month tour in Nam in June 1966 as John and I were graduating from boot camp.

After graduating from boot camp and then ITR (Infantry Training Regiment) at Camp Pendleton, John and I were given 20 days of leave and then ordered to report to Memphis Naval Air Station (MNAS) for aviation training. It was part of the contract we signed to delay the start of boot camp and train for an Aviation MOS (Military Occupational Specialty). When we arrived at Memphis, we started what was called "Zero Week"; a week of aptitude tests where all students were given a chance to select their choice of five desired MOSs. But in the end, it really didn't matter what you wanted, or which MOS you chose, it was what the USMC needed at that time. In the end, we each got what the other had wanted; I immediately started Jet Engine Training and John landed in avionics. Jet engine school started that coming Monday, while John's school started several weeks afterward.

After arriving in Memphis and during any free time, I headed for the basketball courts, my favorite pastime. The base had a large hangar with three full-length courts with pick-up games going on all the time, even in the middle of summer. After a couple of weeks of playing "roundball," I was approached by one of the other guys who had been a regular playing there, and he asked me if I wanted to play for the base team. Of course, I said yes. Little did I know, but he turned out to be the Naval Air Station's executive officer, and the Naval Base's team basketball coach. And as it happened, there were only two students on the team, me and a navy student, a six-foot-three Black kid (Hines) who was very good; everyone else on the team, except for one, were navy regulars. The other was a six-foot-eight Black Marine, and they all were assigned to "Special Services" (primarily they played basketball for the navy).

As students, our classes started at 8am and ended at 4.30pm. Frequently Sloop John B and I were able to get together at the E Club afterward, and then on weekends we would go into the city on liberty, rent a motel room, drink beer and look for the local females. But when basketball season started in mid-October we didn't get to socialize nearly as much. I enjoyed Memphis and the Naval Air Station, and it was great playing on the base team; but the Marine "heavies" did not like me playing on the navy team. And I had "zero duty," which meant that they could not assign me any duty every fourth night, and they didn't like it.

One of the most memorable events that took place while at Memphis was the annual Field Day each November with the Navy vs Marines competing against each other in track and field competition. The Memphis Naval Air Station was the home of several navy air squadrons and the various aviation-related schools. Obviously, it had a much larger naval personnel population, with probably only several hundred Marines, who were primarily aviation students. But the navy made a big deal of it as an annual event. All base personnel and students, along with the numerous navy air squadrons, were required to attend the Field Day, and in winter dress uniform. The air base had a large college-size oval stadium, which was completely full. We Marines were seated together on the opposite side from the announcers, VIPs, and naval officers at mid field; I sat with John and several of his friends.

While everyone was waiting for the dignitaries and general officers to be seated, there was a Marine with the USMC mascot, a bulldog, in front of us on the sideline. The Marine handler was standing at parade rest holding the lease, while the bulldog was just sitting patiently "at ease" next to him. After a few minutes, a sailor with the navy's mascot, a goat, came out from under the stadium seats on the other side of the field. And as they came out onto the field, the goat was fired up trying to head-butt anyone and everyone he could get close to, while the bulldog just sat there at the edge of the field in front of us.

Seeing how feisty the goat was, it wasn't long before many of the navy squids started screaming "Get the dog, get the dog!" We Marines just sat there in silence, not knowing what to expect; that goat was very aggressive and looked very much mean-spirited. But sure enough, with more and more of the navy squids screaming and yelling to "get the dog," it wasn't long before the navy handler and the goat started across the field toward us, and the bulldog.

With the whole stadium of squids egging on the navy handler and the goat, they kept coming closer and closer; and the bulldog just sat there with his front legs bowed in, cool as hell, just staring at the goat. But as the handler and the goat passed the middle of the football field and came about 20 yards from our side, the goat suddenly saw the bulldog, and immediately put its head down, getting ready to charge; and as soon as it did, that dog sprang into action and charged after the goat. The goat suddenly turned, broke free from the handler, and raced to the other side and back in the exit way. We went crazy, yelling, and celebrating as the rest of the stadium fell silent. It was such a gratifying sight to see, and the beginning of a fantastic day for the small group of Marines at MNAS. Our track team creamed the navy in a landslide win; the score was something like 70 to 6.

Initially, at the start of jet engine school and upon graduation, we were told that we would be going straight to helicopter school and then assigned to one of the different types of jet engine helicopters; either to a CH-46, a CH-53, or the Huey school for further helicopter training. However, those plans changed near the end of the jet engine school and most of us Marines in the school were suddenly pulled from the class early, with a different set of orders. We were all headed for WEST-PAC (Vietnam).

Several days before this abrupt change of plans, at about 8pm one evening, Sloop John B and a friend came by my barracks and wanted me to join them at the E Club for a couple of beers. I had just got back from basketball practice, I was dead tired and had just jumped into the rack, so I declined and told him that we would make it happen the next day or on the weekend. Just a couple days later, Friday, we Marines in the jet engine school were given our graduation certificates, along with orders for 20 days' leave, and then ordered to report to Treasure Island Processing Station (near San Francisco) to begin our journey to Nam. Turning down John's invitation for a couple of beers that night became a major regret; it would be the last time I would see Sloop John B.

They must have been preparing our travel orders even before our last week of jet engine school because everything was happening so fast. I should mention that my brother Richard (Dick) and his wife Darlene were also there at Memphis Naval Air Station; Dick had previously enlisted in the navy, and they had recently married. He was also a student there at MNAS; he later became a radar technician aboard a P-3 Orion submarine chaser and surveillance aircraft. I was able to say goodbye to Dick and Darlene but was never able to catch up with Sloop John B or have that final farewell beer.

CHAPTER 3

Off to War

After Memphis, I flew home to Kentucky for 20 days of leave, visiting with my family and friends. But what I remember most was sitting on that airplane at Cincinnati Airport in Covington, Kentucky, waiting to take off for my flight to California: all over the Northern Kentucky area every house was decked out with Christmas lights and decorations, everyone was in the Christmas spirit. It was a cloudy, dark and gloomy late afternoon, only a week from Christmas Day when I already started feeling homesick. I was going off to war and wondering what was in store for me, if I would ever see my family and friends again, and if I would be coming back home. I'm sure that most of the over three million men and women who were sent off to Vietnam had those same feelings. It was not a pleasant day or two of my life.

There were four or five of us Marines together in the jet engine class at Memphis NAS. After our 20 days of leave, we were ordered to report to California, where we were being processed, and wait for our military orders. I believe we were there for two days. I matched up with Pete Harris, who was also from the Cincinnati area; we were given liberty on both evenings, and we had a chance to go see the singer Johnny Rivers at the "Whiskey a Go-Go" in San Francisco, as well as several other bars; and fortunately, we were able to stay out of trouble.

During our time on the west coast, it was not easy to avoid feeling down, wishing that you were back home with your family and friends, especially at that time of year. It was hard not feeling homesick. Those of us Marines who happened to be in the Jet Engine Class really didn't know each other, and now we were among total strangers, mostly Navy, who were working hard to get us on our way to Vietnam, so that they could get home to their loved ones for Christmas.

From Treasure Island, we were transported by bus over to Travis Air Force Base and immediately boarded a civilian airline plane for the flight to Okinawa. It was late at night when the plane took off over the Pacific Ocean, but it seemed like 14 or 15 hours before the sun finally caught up with us. We landed in Japan to refuel the aircraft but were not allowed to get off the plane. However, while sitting there on the tarmac in the early morning sunlight we got an excellent view of Mount Fuji in the background. After refueling, we continued our way to Okinawa.

Our stay at Okinawa was also very brief, for two days as I recall; we arrived mid-morning and received numerous vaccinations, another physical examination, and stored our sea bags with all our Marine dress uniforms. We weren't allowed off base for liberty but were able to go to the Enlisted Club for a couple of beers. We spent the two nights sleeping on cots in the base gymnasium. The next morning we had chow, and were issued jungle utilities and boots, our 782 gear (combat attire, hard hats, flak jackets, and survival belt and knife), our rifles (M14) and a couple of magazines for ammo.

In the early afternoon we boarded a C-130 aircraft which was crammed full of new recruits destined for Vietnam. We landed at Da Nang two or three hours later that afternoon. I thought that being from Kentucky I would have been used to the heat and humidity, but as soon as we stepped off that plane we found out about Vietnam's version of "hot and humid"—even late afternoon in December the temps were over 100 degrees with high humidity.

After a while, as they were sorting out and deciding who was going where, they finally called my name. About 15 of us quickly boarded another aircraft and we flew south to the Marine Air Facility at Chu Lai. The area of the air base was about 3–4 miles of flat sandy soil, and it was located right next to the South China Sea; looking west it was about two miles across before the terrain began to rise up in the mountains. It was the perfect place for the Marine air base, which was the home for two or three fixed-wing attack squadrons. We landed just before dark.

An hour later, those of us destined for helicopters jumped in the back of the 6x6 military truck for the short ride to our new home at MAG 36 (Marine Air Group 36).

It was dark when we left and as soon as we drove through the perimeter of Chu Lai the USMC sergeant in charge barked, "Keep your hard hats on, keep down and stay alert." About 10 minutes later we arrived at the southern gate of Marine Air Group 36 and the helicopter base. We disembarked from the truck and were greeted by the Marine sentries at the fortified bunker/security structure. It was very dark with little lighting, to deny "Charlie" (the Viet Cong) possible targets on the base perimeter. From there we followed a Marine who led the way and continued in the darkness. After a short distance, we came upon the metal tarmac where the helicopters were stored, but it was still too dark to see much of anything. Then suddenly we were greeted by another Marine sentry and his German Shepherd guard dog, which acted and sounded like he would tear your face off, if given the chance. We continued to follow our escort up a slight hill where we came upon rows of living quarters which were referred to as "hooches" (single-story structures made of plywood, on concrete floors). He brought us to an empty hooch which had enough bunks inside for us. It was there that we spent our first night in Vietnam; it was just a few days before Christmas 1966.

At daybreak the next morning we awoke and looked out over the tarmac and the several different types of helicopters which were stationed there at Ky Ha. MAG 36 had three squadrons of helicopters, the CH-34s and CH-46s (both transport helicopters), and the smaller ones, the UH-1E Huey gunships. The one that caught our attention was the Huey, the small one with machine guns pointing outward in all directions. Not sure about the other guys but it was the first time I had ever seen a Huey gunship, or even heard about them.

That morning, those of us from jet engine school were temporarily assigned to the HM&S squadron (Helicopter Marine Maintenance and Support squadron) while they decided which squadron each of us would be assigned to, either the CH-46 or the Huey squadron. (Both helicopters are powered by jet engines.) We were in HM&S for several days. While there, we basically watched while HM&S squadron crews disassembled and/or repaired the jet engines, tested tail rotors, or undertook other maintenance for the helicopter squadrons; but there was only so much that we, the new guys could do. However, they had a small half basketball court in their hangar, and several of us played basketball whenever we got the chance. While there the "heavies" (SNCOs or staff non-commissioned officers) decided that we weren't half bad, and true to the USMC spirit about competition, selected a team and trucked us down to Chu Lai to play a team from the fixed-wing squadrons. I don't remember who won but do remember it being very hot and humid playing on an outside court that day; but it was Vietnam which was hot and humid almost every day.

One of those days in the HM&S hangar while we were playing "roundball" I heard a familiar voice: "Hey Pete." When I looked over, there was Dan Russell. Dan and I had played together in Kentucky on the Dayton High School Green Devils basketball team. Dan had been the star player on our team, and he had been awarded a scholarship to play for Georgia Tech when we were seniors. But suddenly, he was standing there at Ky Ha, and in a Marine uniform. The conversation was so brief, perhaps two to three minutes, that all I got out of it was that the USMC had sent him there by mistake and that he had to run to catch the helicopter that was waiting to take him back to Da Nang. Apparently, he had heard a bouncing basketball, looked in the hangar, and noticed me; but he was in such a hurry to catch his flight, I don't know what happened at Georgia Tech. Nor how he came to be in a Marine uniform; but Vietnam had a way of changing just about every young man's fate, and that was the last that I heard from him. Our conversation was brief, just a few words were all we could manage.

Several days after Christmas 1966, those of us pulled out of the jet engine class were ordered to report to the HM&S Administration Office and informed that we had been assigned to the Huey squadron, VMO-6 (V stands for heavier than Air, M is for Marine, O is Observation). VMO-6 was the oldest helicopter squadron, used mostly in Korea for observation, then for MedeVac missions.

We immediately reported there and found that, like all military services, the USMC divided large units into smaller ones; the Air Wing was divided into squadrons, and our squadron, VMO-6, was broken down into four sections. I was assigned to section 1 and the first hooch, which was for section 1's crew chiefs and us new guys; sections 2, 3 and 4 had their own hooches. Those of us in the first four hooches were lower rank; the SNCOs had their own hooch.

I must admit that the first several weeks in Nam were a culture shock, a wake-up call for me. It was the first of two holiday seasons (Christmas and New Year) in Vietnam; holidays away from family and my friends. There were no holidays in Vietnam for VMO-6, and probably for the other helicopter squadrons for that matter, not even a casual mention of "Merry Christmas" or "Happy Holidays"; it was wartime, and our normal holidays did not exist in Vietnam, at least during my tour.

The mess hall at Ky Ha, location wise, was as good as it gets for Vietnam; it sat high above the beach, with a spectacular view of the South China Sea, and had plenty of seating for the several helicopter squadrons stationed there. However, they forgot about culinary arts. My first breakfast in Nam, I thought the toast was whole grain or wheat bread. Wrong! Somebody mentioned that the flour was left over from World War II, and looking closely at the toast, it was full of baked bugs. Scrambled eggs? They were powdered eggs and came from a can. And the bacon? Greasy bacon, also from a can. It was no big deal to miss breakfast, or lunch for that matter, because when we started flying, we were generally off early and on stand-by at an outlying place, and we mainly lived on C-Rations, which we got used to. As far as food is concerned the only high point that I can remember was midsummer when the whole squadron was available, and we had steaks and cold beer; everything about that was good.

CHAPTER 4

Culture Shock

Upon our arrival in the squadron, like all newcomers in Nam, we were referred to as the FNGs (fucking new guys). Each of us Jet Engine FNGs had been assigned to a veteran crew chief and his bird; my crew chief was Sergeant Johnson. Had we stayed in the States, after graduating from jet engine school, then helicopter training, we would have later been assigned to a squadron stateside, and according to protocol I would have been a "first mech" (mechanic) to a qualified crew chief. Each helicopter would have had an assigned crew chief with a first and maybe a second mech under his supervision for training purposes. But the USMC didn't have that luxury in Nam; there was an acute shortage of flight crews.

For us FNGs, the routine was that we would tag along with our assigned crew chief first thing each morning, but later during the day, while our assigned chief and his bird were off flying somewhere, they would use us to mostly observe and/or help other crews who were repairing "downed" birds, but always under the supervision of the SNCOs. A repair might be replacing a damaged rotor blade, and then "balancing and tracking" the blade, or changing an engine, or whatever part or maintenance the UH-1E Huey needed. That was our "on-the-job training" in Vietnam in 1967. If we had the normal training, we would have received it at the helicopter school back at Memphis.

On New Year's Eve, a little over a week after arriving, we experienced a major typhoon; we spent that afternoon filling and putting more sandbags on the tin roof of our hooch. Fortunately for us in section 1 and our hooch, we survived without any problems, but some of the others were not so lucky with the extremely strong winds and heavy monsoon rains. But when we awoke on New Year's Day, besides some damaged hooches, we discovered that a big US navy ship used to haul supplies, that had been attempting to ride out the typhoon a short distance off the coast, had been blown ashore about 100 yards just to our south. I can only imagine that the skipper on that ship, on New Year's Eve, must have been in big trouble. For months afterward the navy tried in vain to pull it back into the South China Sea at high tide with several other smaller ships and big tugboats; but after a while, they cut the ship in half. They were hoping to haul it off the shore in two sections, but they finally gave up and decided to strap it. Perhaps it is still sitting right there today, just rusting away.

During the first couple weeks in VMO-6, after we tailed along with our assigned crew chief on his pre-flight inspection and then departed Ky Ha for the day, there were several days when they had nothing for us to do, and I got the chance to go swimming and diving on the reef right below the squadron mess hall. At low tide, you could walk out on the reef for about 30 yards; it was amazing to see all the crabs on

Freighter and old LST, Ky Ha.

top of the reef which would jump off in the ocean when I got close to them. The first chance I got to dive in the water next to the reef, it was high tide, and the depth of the water was about 15 feet. I had a diving mask on and everything about the reef and the crystal-clear water was just spectacular, with many different varieties of fish and sea life. However, after an hour or so, I was maybe 30–40 feet from shore, when suddenly I turned a bit and there was a stationary sea snake, just floating there looking back at me. Yes, I hauled ass out of the water. Later that summer, when a friend from Kentucky happened to find me at Ky Ha (see Chapter 11), we did go swimming, my second time, but we stayed away from the reef.

In the first half of my tour, while the squadron was still at Ky Ha, whenever we were flying to or returning from missions from the south, we would fly along the coastline. I used to look down into the crystal-clear water and frequently would see sea turtles and larger fish; from the air, you could see right to the bottom of the ocean. There's no doubt in my mind that there is probably a major resort at Ky Ha today, the shoreline was beautiful and full of sea life.

Several days into the New Year, word came to MAG 36 that the Viet Cong (VC) had raided a nearby Vietnamese village, and had killed the village chief and his family; the village was just south of the Marine Air Base at Chu Lai. Supposedly they hung his body up at the entrance of the village. A couple days later, the VC attacked the South Korean Marine base camp, which was in the same area as the above-mentioned village. The Korean camp was just 5–10 miles south of the Chu Lai Air Base and was part of their TAOR (territorial area of responsibility). During that night we were fully aware that there was something big going on, as the squadron gunships and the CH-34 transports were busy all night. That next morning, we FNGs went out to the flight line to discover a badly shot up CH-34 sitting out of the way near the "takeoff and landing strip" with dozens and dozens of bullet holes in it; even the two rubber tires on the 34 were flat from enemy fire. While we were still counting bullet holes, another 34 carrying more Korean WIAs (wounded in action) landed nearby and started unloading more wounded Koreans. One of the wounded Koreans jumped out of the helicopter and was walking on his own power; he was carrying his rifle with one hand, but under that arm, he had the lower part of his heavily bandaged other severed arm. He was obviously sky-high on morphine and other medication that the navy corpsmen had given him, but apparently, he refused to be carried on a stretcher, insisting on walking on his own power. In fact, as he walked by us, it must have been obvious to him that we were new in Nam; probably our eyes were as big as saucers with shock, but he was so "out of it" with the meds they had given him, he was showing off how bad he was, and trying to intimate us newbies, and he somewhat did; we thought by the way he was acting that he may have wanted to fight us. At any rate, this was before we FNGs had even been in-country for maybe two weeks.

There were 12,000 helicopters shot down during the Vietnam War. I believe that most of them were powered by jet engines; only one (that I am aware of) ran on gasoline: the CH-34. While I was in Nam, VMO-6 worked many, many missions with the CH-34 and I found it amazing how much battle damage those helicopters could sustain and continue to fly. This is in no way to diminish the role of the rest of CH-53, CH-46, or the Huey helicopters, but if one enemy bullet found its way into the jet engine, we would be going down. But the "Ugly Angel" (and I mention that name for the benefit of all the 34 squadrons)

This CH-34 has seen some action!

was powered by a nine-cylinder gasoline engine, and I was told that incredibly, a CH-34 would continue to fly with only two cylinders still operating. And in the first two weeks of my time in Nam and seeing those two CH-34s bringing in those WIAs and KIAs, I found it just unbelievable how much damage those two helicopters had sustained, and were still able to fly back to base. To say nothing about the courage of the Marine CH-34 crews, and their WIAs and KIAs, who were on those missions. Those Korean Marines were such fierce fighters. Rumor had it that during that night attack, the enemy penetrated the perimeter wire, and the Koreans pulled the wire back together so that the invading VC could not escape. Then it was all hand-to-hand fighting. For us FNGs, only two weeks in the country, this was all a real eye-opener, but only the beginning of what was in store for us in the next year.

Shortly after I arrived in the squadron, a couple of the Koreans would come to our hooch about once or twice a week and ask us if we would buy items for them at the camp PX. Ky Ha was located on a peninsula. There was a large body of water to the northwest that emptied into the South China Sea. At the north end at Ky Ha the channel was deep enough for the navy transport ships to enter and unload supplies for the Marine Air Base, MAG 36 and the Koreans. I believe that the navy ship that was washed ashore New Year's Eve was trying to ride out the storm when they had their mishap. No doubt the Koreans who were unloading supplies were some of the ones who were asking us to buy things for them, because they were not allowed to buy anything at our camp PX. Anyway, we became friends with them and would go to the exchange and get them the items they wanted, which were mostly electronic goods. After I started flying, I didn't see much of them, but the other guys in the hooch helped them out, and it seemed to be harmless courtesy for our Korean friends. Also, toward the north end of Ky Ha near the unloading dock, there was a small chapel for Sunday services. I don't recall seeing any other religious facilities on US bases or camps in my travels in Nam, but I was able to attend my one and only Mass there.

During that January, we FNGs hung around the squadron area sometimes helping, but mostly observing others on the flight line working on their birds. At the end of the day, we would wait in the ready hooch for our crew chief and his bird to return from missions or from standby duty at outlying points. When they finally came back, we would go out and assist the crew chief, observe him inspecting his bird, help him put away the door guns, assist him putting on the plastic gun and door covers to keep the rain out, and/or help with whatever he wanted. When all that was done, we would run off to the mess hall for some chow.

One day late in the afternoon Sergeant Johnson and the crew arrived back at Ky Ha, and the pilots and the gunner went off in different directions. As I was approaching his bird, Johnson came walking toward me, looking very upset. When we met, the only thing he said was, "Clean up that mess," and kept walking. When I got to the bird and looked inside, the floor was covered with blood. It took many buckets of water to get rid of the blood. A short time later he came back, started his "post-flight" inspection, and we finished buttoning up the bird for the night. Nothing was said about what had happened and I figured I'd just leave it alone. But it was obvious that they had picked up a badly wounded WIA, or a KIA.

My time with Sergeant Johnson was very limited. He was a Black man and a very quiet person; we did not converse a lot. I attributed it to his flight schedule—he was flying almost every day, so we didn't have much time together. I don't think it was anything racial because there were several other Black Marines in the squadrons, and they all seemed to be very friendly and popular. I also remember the issue was brought up in boot camp: "There are no Black or white Marines, we are all Marines, and we wear green uniforms, and we all bleed red." Whether or not that holds true elsewhere in the Corps, I don't know. But mostly I conceded that the difference between Johnson and I was the difference in rank; I was a lowly lance corporal and an "FNG"; he was a sergeant and a "short-timer," getting ready to rotate home.

Several days later, in mid-January, there were three of us FNGs in the ready hooch just hanging around with nothing to do. Suddenly, the gunnery sergeant came charging in and shouted, "I need three volunteers, you, you and you. Go get your '782' gear, your rifles and two magazines of ammo, and be back here in zero five." Five minutes later we were back, and we had no idea of what was up. Then, in a couple more minutes, the gunny came running back in and told us we were going to get on that "slick"—a Huey, with doors still on, and no ordnance attached—that they were getting ready out on the flight line, and going for a ride. Right behind the gunny was Sergeant Johnson, who wasn't flying that day. It really surprised me when he came up to me, put his hand on my shoulder, looked me in the eye, and said, "Keep your damn head down." It was the most conversation that I had ever had with him in our short time together. It would be the last time I would see Sergeant Johnson. I didn't realize it, but he rotated home later that day.

A minute or so later, the crew chief on the Huey slick came running into the hooch yelling, "You ready? Let's go." The three of us hurried behind him and jumped in the bird. We taxied out on the runway, got clearance to depart, and took off, still having no idea what was happening or where we were going. The three of us didn't have flight helmets, so couldn't hear any radio communications. But after a short ride to the south, as we were circling around what was obviously a big battle on the ground, suddenly the crew chief yelled at us to take off our hard hats and sit on them because the "gooks" were shooting at us. Prior to taking off our hard hats, the only thing that we could hear was the whine of the jet engine, and the "wop-wop" of the helicopter blades. It was the first time that any of us would be getting close to the action and getting shot at, and only the beginning of discovering what it was like flying around in the sky.

Fortunately, we landed in the middle of a large dried-up rice paddy, but I don't think that we had taken any hits. The Huey slick landed, and then took off as soon as we jumped out. We were in the middle of a heated battle in the general area south of where the Korean Marines' camp was located, and where the VC had attacked the Vietnamese village previously mentioned; perhaps 5–6 miles south of the Chu Lai airfield. There were fire fights all around us and we could hear all the sounds of battle; however, we were in a safe location near the makeshift command post. There were a couple of sections of squadron gunships pounding the surrounding area with machine guns and rockets blasting away at the enemy. All three of us were wide awake.

We discovered the reason we were there. If one of our gunships was shot down, then we were supposed to go out and help secure the downed bird, help rig it up so that it could be lifted off the battlefield by one of the big CH-53s, then haul it back to Ky Ha. Thinking back, I strongly suspect that if a gunship had been shot down and we had gone out to get that bird out of there, it probably would have been a fiasco as we were so inexperienced, especially standing up on top of a downed Huey with Viet Cong bullets flying all around us.

If one of our birds had been shot down, and knowing what I know now, I suspect the CH-53, while hovering overhead, would have dropped a cable down and we would have wrapped it around the rotor head and off it would go. Fortunately, none of our birds were downed that day, and none of us even had to fire our weapons. At the end of the day we returned to Ky Ha and started to calm down, thinking about what could have happened but probably picturing ourselves as heroes. Right! But it was our first taste of being near the action in Nam.

Mid-January, with a couple other squadron mates, I was given a three-hour pass to go off base to visit a small Vietnamese village which was less than a mile from the north perimeter gate. I was told that they had cold beer there, plus I wanted to buy a pair of what we called "tiger paws"—like flip-flops here in the States, which the local villagers made from old automobile tires with the straps out of old inner tubes. January was monsoon season and it rained just about every day. We wore hard hats and ponchos, and carried our M-14s with live rounds, though it was relatively safe and as far as I knew nobody ever got in trouble in that village.

The village was very primitive, as was most of Vietnam in the I Corps area. After a short walk we came upon some small hooches with open windows, tin roofs, and straw walls, and found the "Manasan" who was selling the tiger paws. In front of her hooch there was a glass display case with the footwear. Standing next to the display case there were three little kids barefoot, shivering in the cold damp weather with very little clothing on. I ended up buying a pair of size 12 tiger paws, plus three smaller pairs for the three kids, for the equivalent of about $10.

We continued our way until we got to the center of the village and the local pub hooch which sold beer. I think that the beer was called "Tiger 7" and it was indeed cold, and tasted very good. I think the "7" must have been for the alcohol content because after downing two beers

I was feeling a buzz. At any rate, time passed by quickly and our passes were good from noon to 1500 hours, so we decided we better head back to base. On the way back, there were the same three little kids standing out in the cold and rain, barefoot again, with their tiger paws back in the display case. But to be honest, I don't remember being mad. Unless you were there, you can't imagine the daily hardship that most of the Vietnamese people had to endure, and they did what they had to do to survive. That three-hour base liberty would be my only opportunity to socialize with local Vietnamese people.

A couple of days later, I was sitting on my cot writing a letter home, when several of my squadron mates came back into the hooch after being on liberty off base in the village that I had previously visited. They were taking off their ponchos and gear and putting up their rifles; I wasn't paying any attention to them, writing my letter; when I heard, "Hey Greene," and looked up. There was one of the guys just returning, standing in front of me with his rifle pointing right at me. I just said, "Knock it off, cut the shit," and went back to writing. Suddenly, we heard a gunshot, and there was the same guy, a sergeant, soon to be busted down to corporal, looking very embarrassed. Seconds later, several "heavies," who had heard the shot, came running into the hooch to investigate. Fortunately for me, he had lifted the rifle up a little before he pulled the trigger. The bullet went over my head and out through the roof. Perhaps he had had too many of those "Tiger 7" beers?

About a week later, again I was sitting on my cot writing a letter, when two of the guys were coming back from the mess hall; one of them yelled, "Greene, look down." When I looked down between my legs, there was a giant black spider crawling under my cot; that damn spider was as big as my fist, and its legs were as long as my fingers. I don't know if he was going to bite me or not, but I know for a fact, that day I did my highest vertical leap ever.

Later, in midsummer, we had a huge monsoon storm during the night. When we got up that next morning to start pre-flighting our birds for the day's activities, the storm was over and the sun was coming out; but all over the flight deck where all the helicopters were parked, there were hundreds and hundreds of giant Asian beetles, as big as a closed fist.

They somehow had been caught up in the storm and were swept away from wherever they came from and littered most of the flight line at Ky Ha. They were all dying or dead. We had to watch our step making our way out to our birds. I remember later that afternoon when we got back from outlying points, the guys who were not flying that day must have swept them up and loaded them in the bucket of the tractor, and I suppose that they dumped them in the ocean. It was the only time that I saw one of those giant spiders, or the Asian beetles; but one thing for sure, Vietnam was a different place. I can only imagine what the Marines on the ground (the grunts) had to deal with out in the bush and back in the jungles of Nam: not only the spiders and beetles but all the other bugs and insects, the leeches, and the ferocious mosquitoes that drove me crazy early on when I first arrived in Nam. The grunts had to cope with all those things, not to mention "Charlie," the Viet Cong, and the NVA.

CHAPTER 5

A Brief History of VMO-6

Originally formed in April 1945, VMO-6 was the oldest helicopter squadron of the USMC. The squadron arrived in Vietnam in the fall of 1965, was briefly based at Da Nang, then relocated to the small helicopter base at Ky Ha. From what I understand, when VMO-6 put down its roots at Ky Ha, the squadron was short on pilots, aircrew, and other maintenance personnel. Everything about the squadron was changing, from older aircraft and helicopters to Bell Helicopters' new UH-1E Huey. Bell had several versions of the Huey which were used by the US Army, but the UH-1E is the shorter version and became the USMC's new aircraft which was modified to become the Marine Huey gunship.

During the Vietnam War, the Marine Corps had about 15 helicopter squadrons situated at various points in the I Corps area, the northern portion of South Vietnam. The squadrons were made up of CH-53s, CH-46s, CH-34s, and the UH-1E Huey; some were located at Ky Ha, Marble Mountain at Da Nang, and at Phu Bai. In addition, there were 46 and 34 squadrons stationed aboard (older) navy carriers that were repurposed for helicopters, and they were stationed just off the coast out on the South China Sea. Before I arrived in Nam, VMO-6 and its gunships were already operating on a steady diet of combat missions, and the squadron had suffered KIAs, many WIAs, and had already lost several of its UH-1E Hueys. During Vietnam, the basic role of the gunship squadrons was to protect the transport helicopters during medevac missions, troop insertions and extractions, resupply missions, and support the Marines on the ground during operations and out on patrols. Basically, whenever the Marines or South Vietnamese friendlies (RVN) got in trouble, the gunships were dispatched to support them. And there weren't many days when the gunships were not busy. Someone was always in trouble.

At Ky Ha, first thing in the morning, the daily routine for VMO-6 would be to disperse a "section" (two gunships) to various points in the southern portion of the I Corps area to respond when Marines got in trouble. The first gunship would be assigned as the medevac escort, which would be partnered up with a transport chopper, generally a CH-34. Then the next two gunships would be on standby duty at Ky Ha, followed by a section of guns that would be sent to a small airfield west of the town of Tam Ky for standby. Frequently, two gunships would be sent out aboard one of the navy helicopter carriers in the South China Sea for the day, and sometimes longer for standby duty; and frequently a section of gunships would be sent up to Da Nang to help VMO-2, and up to Phu Bai to assist VMO-3.

A note of interest: the USMC is noted for being competitive, even within itself; for me it started in boot camp between the squads within the platoon, and then our platoon #178 competing against the other platoons within our company for first-place finishes. There were perhaps 10 different flags that each platoon was competing for. And finally, we competed to see which platoon was #1, the Honor Platoon, at graduation time. That competition continued even among the various helicopter squadrons, and I'm sure that was the case within the CH-34s and 46s. Quite frequently, at least for me, whenever we were sent TAD (temporary assigned duty) up to Marble Mt. (Da Nang) to assist VMO-2, our gunships would sit at the very northern end of their flight mat, far away from VMO-2's ready hooch and their flight crews. There was no camaraderie between VMO-2 and VMO-6, at least from what I observed. While I was there at Marble Mt., when we were assigned missions they came directly from "Land Shark" or VMO-2 radio communications. I don't recall any person-to-person conversation with VMO-2's pilots or the flight crews, we generally just stayed with our birds waiting to receive mission assignments. However, there is a difference between comradery and rivalry, and as far as I recall there was no combination of VMO-2 and VMO-6 working together on specific missions.

When we were TAD at Marble Mt., we were their rivals; and much like a basketball game, when the game was over, we could still be comrades. And when Marines were in trouble, whether on the ground, or if one of their gunships had been shot, "esprit de corps" would have kicked in and we came together, even if it meant risking your life.

It was during those "down" times, waiting between missions, time permitting, that I was able to grab my camera and take pictures of the fixed-wing aircraft taking off on the north end of the Da Nang airport runway, and once or twice I was able to walk through the perimeter guard gate and across the street to an area the Marines there called "Dog Patch." Dog Patch was the southern part of the city of Da Nang, inhabited by the local Vietnamese, who had several shops there selling their merchandise. Our two birds were only about 20 yards away from the north perimeter and when given the opportunity, I grabbed the camera and took pictures, but always on the alert to run back when we received a new mission.

CHAPTER 6

Time to Start Flying

When I arrived in Nam, I really had no idea what exactly was in store for me, I knew nothing about helicopters, nor realized the extent of the role that they would play in the Vietnam War. It was the morning after arrival at Ky Ha when I got my first glimpse of a Huey gunship, and I recall that the other FNGs who arrived with me were also in awe when we saw it for the first time. I could have ended up in a CH-46 squadron, or even stayed in the H&MS working on jet engines, but I ended up where I wanted to be, VMO-6. Later in life it occurred to me, that at least for me, it had been a waste of time sending us to jet engine school at Memphis. Yes, we learned about vanes and struts, the three parts of a jet engine and the basics of how a jet engine works, but I never had to work on the jet engines on the three birds that I had, and I never had to pull the engine out of any of my birds; they all worked fine without me screwing them up. And yes, it would have been better if we had been able to continue on to helicopter school at Memphis, but at least for me, it all worked out.

Early every morning we were up with our crew chief for that day, and we would follow him around on his inspection routine and try to absorb as much information as we could. The first order of business on the helicopter's daily pre-flight inspection list was to get a fuel sample. The fuel tank on the Huey is right behind the crew chief's side, the left side of the bird. There is a small release valve on the bottom of the tank under the bird; we would push the valve up to let a little bit of JP-4 fuel and any condensation (water) flow out, then hold the glass jar under again to catch a sample of JP-4. Each bird had a numbered jar on the display rack right outside of the "ready" hooch so the pilots could see that there was no water in it.

After the fuel sample, next we would check the nose compartment of the bird where most of the avionics were located. Then we would jump in the pilot's seat to check to see if the battery and all the instrument gauges were working. Everything OK there, we would work our way down the right side of the bird checking the compartment behind the gunner's seat, where the hydraulic tanks and gauges for the transmission were located, then open the cowlings and continue checking the right side of the engine and inspect the length of drive shaft and the bearings from the transmission to the tail rotor. Then the left side of the bird and that side of the engine, then climb up to the top of the bird to inspect all the different bearings and the main rotor head.

After the inspections, both pre-flight and post-flight, or after any repairs that were made, the crew chief would sign off the bird as "up," available for service. Prior to flying the Huey, the pilot would also perform a pre-flight as well; basically, the same procedure as the crew chief. This is what the crew chief and pilots did several times a day to avoid falling out of the sky. And this was the beginning of my 13-month tour in VMO-6 in Vietnam.

Before my arrival at VMO-6, the UH-1E had been transformed from passenger service to gunship status; the two back doors had been removed, and the squadron metal workers prefabricated and installed outside outriggers which held up the two external M-60 machine guns, and a rocket launcher pod on each side of the Huey. Staff Sergeant Witham (who Rod Croft and I became good friends with after Vietnam) had had a major role in these adaptations. While at Ky Ha, they generally kept one Huey intact with the rear doors, which they referred to as a slick; it was used primarily for VIP flights, possible emergency medevac extractions, or transporting replacement parts.

There were two sizes of rocket pods that were used on the gunships; generally, the smaller pods were used because of weight considerations, each holding seven HE (high explosive) rockets; but occasionally the larger pods were used, depending on the situation. The larger pods each held 19 rockets. A fully loaded Huey gunship had four external M-60 machine guns and either 14 or 38 rockets which shot straight ahead. With the back doors removed the crew chief and gunner each operated another M-60 so in total the gunship would carry 10–12,000 rounds of 7.62mm ammo when we departed on missions. Later in the year, the squadron installed the Tat 101 on the nose of several of the gunships, including mine, WB#1. The Tat 101 comprised twin M-60s that fired simultaneously, hydraulically operated, and used by the co-pilot. This gave a total of eight M-60 machine guns, each firing 500 rounds per minute. However, in my opinion, the Tat 101 was a waste of time, and added more weight to the bird, because I can't remember a co-pilot ever using the Tat 101 in combat; the only time was when they tried to get familiar with it. But when the bullets started flying the co-pilot was busy enough with the normal duties required in a fire fight. The pilots didn't like it because it was extra weight and made the nose of the bird heavier.

The makeup of the aircrew on the Huey in VMO-6 was the pilot, co-pilot, crew chief, and gunner. The pilot was in charge, sat up front in the right seat, and generally was the senior officer. New pilots in the squadron were in the left seat next to the pilot. The crew chief sat behind the co-pilot on the left side of the bird, with the gunner behind the pilot on the right side. The crew chief and the gunner basically performed the same functions during flight; they were responsible for protecting their side of the bird from enemy fire, especially after pulling out of a rocket or strafing run when the gunships were most vulnerable, when they were "low and slow"; and just as important, keeping the door and exterior machine guns working. Generally, the gunners had a different MOS: they were avionics, ordnance, clerks, etc., and/or the "heavies" (NCOs, senior enlisted) from within the squadron. They did not fly every day, but shared gunner's duties sporadically when they wanted to fly.

It was two or three weeks into January '67 when we FNGs started being assigned as gunners on the daily schedule. But once we started flying, it was practically every day; I don't remember having time off except if my bird was down and needed repair.

The crew chiefs were helicopter mechanics originally, who had then been promoted to that status. Once someone had gained the status of crew chief, he was assigned his own bird, and was responsible for the upkeep and maintenance of that bird. Crew chiefs performed all the inspections on their Huey each day; before, during, and after flights. They performed whatever maintenance that was required, including replacing parts, such as a rotor blade, tail rotor, drive shaft, or any number of parts. Whenever a part was replaced and/or major maintenance was performed, then afterward the bird was required to be taken on a test flight for a safety check. During the test "hop" the crew chief would sit in the co-pilot's seat to assist and answer the test pilot if he had any concerns or inquiries about the bird. And generally, once the test pilot had completed the test routine, he would pass the controls to the crew chief while he was filling out the necessary paperwork. (I understand that early on after the squadron arrived in-country, there was such a shortage of pilots for some of the missions, that on occasion, some of the more experienced crew chiefs would even fly as the co-pilots on combat missions.)

The Marine Corps used the term "crew chief" on its helicopters and other aircraft, and the term could imply overseeing the operational flight crew, but that was not the case for us. In VMO-6 the crew chief was charged with keeping the bird in good working order; and when it was not, the crew chief had the authority to "down" the aircraft, and then report it to his section leader and/or to one of the squadron's senior NCOs. That was the extent of his authority as a crew chief on a VMO-6 Huey gunship.

In fact, like most of the other crew chiefs during Nam, because of the rapid development and deployment of helicopter use there, when I was assigned my first bird I was a "provisional" crew chief, a lowly lance corporal and (I became a corporal later in my tour). It was in June 1967 when I was certified and received my official title as crew chief on a UH-1E Huey gunship. Even then, most generally, I was junior in rank on any given day; the gunner on my right side much of the time was senior in rank. The pilot in the right seat was in command of my bird in flight, and if we were the "lead" gunship, he was in command of the crew, the flight, and most of the missions that we flew that day.

During my tour, from December '66 thru January '68, the squadron had three commanding officers (COs), Lieutenant Colonels Maloney,

Sign at Phu Bai.

Nelson, and White; the COs rotated every six months. All three of our COs were "hands-on," they flew frequently, and they knew all the flight crews. They were just like the other pilots, treated everyone with respect, didn't have an attitude nor were on an ego trip. We were all there to do our jobs: protect the transport helicopters, take care of the Marines on the ground, watch each other's backs, and try to get back safely in one piece.

Another thing I liked about VMO-6 was that there didn't seem to be any "I'm an officer and you are an enlisted man" or "I am your superior and you do what I say" mentality. We crew chiefs were somewhat treated as equals. I would say "Good morning, Sir," and the CO would reply, "Good morning, Lance Corporal," or later, "Corporal." (Unlike screens shown in the movies about Navy fighter pilots gathered in their ready rooms when the Commanding Officer walks in.). I don't ever remember that when the CO walked into the "ready room hooch," or who happened to be flying that day when someone would cry out "ATTENTION" and everyone in the hooch jumped up and stood at attention. It was that way with each of the COs we had while I was there. On any given day it could have been Lieutenant Colonel Maloney, or Lieutenant Colonel Nelson, who we affectionately referred to as "Crazy Joe," and later Lieutenant Colonel White who might have been the pilot on your bird that day. All of them treated us crew chiefs with the same respect that they did the other officers/pilots; we were all on the same team. Each and every one of us crew chiefs was able to sit back and observe the talent, the decision-making, and the bravery of the pilots of VMO-6 that we flew with daily. I truly regret not finishing the book earlier because I would have like to have acknowledged all three of our commanding officers. I'm pleased to be able to include part of Lieutenant Colonel Nelson's story in his own words:

> In VMO-6, I had fifty young pilots, and about a hundred dedicated young, enlisted troops on the side guns. Most of my plane captains were lads only eighteen or nineteen years old. They were the most loyal Marines I had known in any war. All these plane captains insisted on flying as side door gunners whenever their plane flew. Most of the planes in my squadron flew approximately ten hours a day, usually under enemy fire. These young men would work at night to maintain their birds, sometimes going without sleep or even food until the plane was ready to go again, and when it launched, they were in the side door with their M-60 Machine guns as well as another young man in the other door.
>
> At Ky Ha we were fortunate in that the enemy-harassing rockets were never fired at our base. Da Nang and Phu Bai areas had nightly problems with incoming rockets, which affected their ability to work at night on their planes. So, their availability at times was low. My squadron, however, was able to maintain at least 10–12 birds flying every day, for an average of more than five thousand combat hours each month.
>
> The loyalty and hard work, patriotism, and dedication of every man in VMO-6, was the greatest thing I had known in my entire career. What a privilege it was to work with these lads each day, regardless of the dangers of combat. I never had to ask for volunteers to go with me on dangerous missions. One, Lance Corporeal Arthur Friend, age eighteen, from Louisiana, was typical.
>
> On a dark and stormy night about 0100, I was working through all the paperwork in my VMO-6 office, when an emergency call came in from Crankcase 3 with First Recon (a nine-man team) saying that they were surrounded by a large enemy force and under heavy fire. They were surrounded by unknown enemy numbers out near Ho Chi Minh's trail over in the mountains to the west. (We kept a special radio in our ready room to hear the whispers of the Recon Teams when they were in trouble, to expedite our help.)
>
> As I went out to get on my airplane, it was one that had been shot up several days before, and the loyal young Lance Corporal about 18 years old who was the plane captain, was there, and he helped me strap in, ready to "go to war." He was an unusually sharp young man, gifted with common sense, and a deadeye shot with his M-60 in the side door. This young man had voluntarily worked on the plane for two days and two nights without relief or sleep, patching the

holes and cleaning the plane up getting it ready. I don't know if the lad had even stopped for food. His eyes were red, and he looked fatigued.

I told the OPS officer to get me another man to take his place with the side door machine gun, because this was going to be a very dangerous night, and he probably wouldn't be able to survive if we went down out there in enemy country. So, I asked for a replacement for him on the side door. As we hurriedly got ready for takeoff, I was making the last-minute checks in the right seat (which is first pilot for helicopters) when the young plane captain with blood shot eyes came over and tapped me on the shoulder and said, "Skipper, he's got to whip my fanny to take my place. It's my plane. I fix it, I'll fly."

I said to my co-pilot, "We have about two hundred of these here in our Band of Brothers in VMO-6, and each one is special to me." I told the lad, "O.K., get in, and let's go to war." It was about 0130 when we took off. I was kind of glad to have that youngster with me because this mission was considered life or death for the Recon Team, and he could be trusted in his orientation never to endanger the friendlies, so I could allow him to have "free guns" on his side. Such was the case with the loyalty of every man in my squadron.

The weather was down to the ground and pouring down rain. We had to proceed under a low hanging ceiling along with the CH-46 rescue helicopter. To get there, we had to go down a dry riverbed in the mountains, at about 50 feet altitude, to stay under the low hanging ceiling. After arriving at the Recon team, the CH-46 had to hover in the treetops to lift each man out by cable.

I circled the CH-46 in a right-hand turn and let the side gunner spray the area around the team below to discourage the enemy from their intent. I circled as close to the hovering CH-46 as I could to draw enemy fire, which would help the CH-46 to survive in its hover, and my side gunner would strafe in an arc as we circled. The cloud overhead was practically in the treetops also! When he'd run out of ammunition, the right-hand gunner would furnish him with more ammo. L/Cpl. Friend was able to quiet the enemy down with his M-60 and made the rescue possible. On the way out, we had to go up the dry riverbed, the way we had come in, and then cross a 400-foot ridge that was now enshrouded in clouds. This made for an anxious several minutes until we could let down on the other side over the rice paddies, hoping to get back in the clear from the storm. Fortunately, we had approximately fifty feet of ceiling over the rice paddies near the coast and completed our homeward bound journey. And so, we brought the Recon team home safely, regardless of the weather.

Arthur G. Friend, crew chief for Lieutenant Colonel Nelson on this flight, recalls:

After the CO directed my gunner to fire at the enemy locations, he would not because he was afraid because of the enemy's closeness to the recon team. So, I got on my gunner's M-60 machine gun and commenced delivering withering fire upon the seven (7) automatic weapons that were firing on our recon team. The other Huey gunbird also would not fire because they were of the same contention about the closeness of the enemy to the team. As LtCol Nelson would reverse his orbit around the team's position, I would move from the right-side gunners gun to my own M-60. At times I would remove either my gun or my gunners so that I might train upon the enemy. Although not an approved procedure, I would shoot between the belly of the Huey and its skids and or farther behind the external guns and rocket pods to remain on target.

When the first CH-46 was utilizing their external hoist to lift the first person who happened to be the Navy Corpsman the hoist cable broke, and he fell 75–80 feet to his death. That was the only KIA victim for this recon team. The other CH-46 did not have a rescue hoist installed so we had to wait for a replacement to be sent from Ky Ha. This replacement helo was able to successfully retrieve the remainder of the team.

My efforts resulted in silencing all seven (7) of the enemy's automatic weapons which allowed the replacement CH-46 to make recovery of the recon team without receiving any battle damage.

Nelson continues:

There were many such emergency evacuations that Art Friend joined me as my side gunner. On another trip, when we got back, I looked the plane over, and there was a big patch of blood near the left door. I asked Friend about it, and why he didn't tell me that he had been hit. He said he was hit earlier in the day, and that the bullet had cut about a two-inch gash in the right cheek of his fanny. He said that would be his fourth "Purple Heart" and he did not want anybody to know about it because four Purple Hearts would cause him to be transferred from combat. He said, "Besides, Skipper, I knew you needed me."

I was able to attend his retirement party, and I noticed his uniform still bore his four Purple Hearts from VMO-6 along with a chest full of combat ribbons from Vietnam. Art Friend had not wanted to tell me about his fourth Purple Heart, because he was afraid that I'd send him home. I now realize that this command was the greatest privilege and challenge of my entire thirty-two years in my Marine Corps career.

★★★

Our home at Ky Ha, when I first arrived, was small with limited space compared to the other two Marine Corps helicopter bases (Marble Mountain and Phu Bai), or the big US Army base to the south in the II Corps area. Initially, the three squadrons at Ky Ha were closely bunched together with CH-34 and CH-46 helicopters, although later the transport squadrons were transferred out aboard the helicopter carriers at sea for a period. At the southern end of the flight line there was a runway for takeoffs and landings. Whenever the Hueys taxied from our parking spaces to the takeoff/landing strip when departing Ky Ha, the heavily loaded gunships with rockets and external machine guns would have to sit down on the takeoff strip facing out at the ocean before "arming/activating" the bird's external weapons on the takeoff runways. It was certainly not safe for a couple of gunships to be taxiing around at 2–3 feet off the deck among the other parked helicopters with "activated" rockets and machine guns.

Marine Air Group MAG 36 at Ky Ha was by far the safest base for helicopters; 75 percent of the base was surrounded by water. Looking north, the South China Sea was on the right side, to the north was a wide river and the harbor, then open water to the northwest. Helicopter repair was a 24/7 operation. I can recall only two or three mortar attacks, but they were mostly for harassment. The only injury that I can recall was one of the "heavies" got some shrapnel in his buttocks trying to get into his bunker. But that changed drastically when the squadron moved north to Quang Tri in September '67. I'm told that the squadron originally had 24 UH-1E Hueys; however, while at Ky Ha we generally only had half that many available for service, in the "up" status. It seemed that there were always 4–5 birds sitting off to the side (in the "graveyard") covered up with an old parachute awaiting replacement parts, some of them being cannibalized for parts to keep the other birds flying.

On my maiden flight as a gunner, I climbed aboard the Huey on the right side behind the pilot; the crew chief was outside holding one of the rotor blades, waiting for the pilot's cue to release it. When the blade was freed the crew chief jumped aboard and the pilot started the engine, got up to full engine power and rotor speed, then slowly lifted the helicopter to about 2–3 feet off the deck and we taxied away from the squadron's parking area, followed by the chase bird. Out on the short runway/takeoff strip we sat back down looking out over the open water.

The crew chief and I then got out, inserted the barrels into the external machine guns, and then connected the electrical wire and the female plug into the receptacle on top of the rocket pod so that the pod could be energized, "hot." After I connected the electrical plug, I started to screw the threaded coupler of the plug onto the male part of the pod receptacle when the crew chief yelled, "Don't screw it on." I asked why, but we were in a hurry, and all he said was "You'll find out, I'll tell you later," so we jumped in, hooked up our safety belts, and took off.

Later that day the crew chief explained that if by chance, and it does happen on occasion, one of the rockets gets stuck inside the rocket pod after it has been fired, the pod needs to be jettisoned. That rocket having been activated (fired), the rear propellant portion of the rocket starts burning toward the warhead and is trying to propel the rocket forward toward the target. When that propellant reaches the warhead, it will explode on the side of the bird. You are in real trouble if, after the pilot has tried to jettison the rocket pods, one of them is still tangling under the bird by the electrical cord because you have screwed on the female plug onto the male receptacle.

If there is a "fired" rocket still lodged in the pod, as a safety feature, the pilot would pull a release lever located between their seats, and both pods would fall away. The release lever between the pilots' seats was hooked up to a cable pulley system which was located under the helicopter floor and worked its way to each of the rocket pod support systems on the outriggings. But as a backup, either the crew chief or the gunner could reach out and manually pull the release lever outside on the gun rack on his side. Obviously, it was an infrequent occurrence, but not infrequent enough as far as I am concerned, because that crew chief was right. That scenario happened to me three or four times in the following months; the first couple times, a "fired" rocket was stuck in the pod and the pilot pulled the emergency release lever and both pods fell away. Apparently, all the crew chiefs probably have had those same episodes at some time during their tours, it was just an infrequent event that we dealt with.

But the last time it happened it was quite a bit different. We were out on a mission supporting the grunts with bullets flying. We were in a rocket run when one of the rockets on my side became stuck in the pod. The pilot pulled the emergency release lever and the pod on the gunner's side fell off, but not the one on my side. I reached out to manually release it, only to discover that both the front and back of the lever were caked with wet sand, the lever was stuck, preventing it from moving back and releasing the pod. The open slot for the pod release lever on the outrigging was only about ¾ inch high by about 1½ inch long, just enough room to stick the tip of your finger in, to pull the lever back and manually let the pod fall away.

I could easily reach out to my side of the lever but couldn't get it to move because of all the sand caked around it, and I had to take off my safety belt to get out far enough. There was only about a ¼ inch of space in the front and rear of the lever, and I wasn't getting much of the sand out. Panic was starting to set in as that rocket propellant must have been getting close to the warhead. Finally, I crawled out onto the top of the supporting gun rack, straddling it with a leg on each side. I started digging with my right- and left-hand fingers on both sides and both front and back of the release lever, that's when I realized that everyone in the bird was screaming at me, "Greene, hurry up, hurry the fuck up!"

I was pushing down on the pod with both feet and digging with my fingers on both sides of the lever, when finally, the pod and burning rocket fell away. I remember putting the front of my flight helmet down on the gun rack, giving a sigh of relief, and saying to myself, "Thank you Lord." But after a couple more seconds, I suddenly realized that my legs and feet were just hanging there, with nothing under them. I was out there on the outrigging and the gun rack without the safety belt on, and we were about several hundred feet above the ground. I scrambled back inside the bird. There was no question, everyone aboard was greatly relieved that we were not going to blow up.

That crew chief several months earlier was exactly right, and I have wondered how many of the other crew chiefs had anything close to that event. As far as the sand that was caked on in the release lever slot, the only thing that I could think of was it had been raining, and it rained a lot over there, and we must have picked up the sand when we landed on the ground somewhere other than a metal flight deck. And we must have been away from Ky Ha the previous night because the ordnance guys would have blasted clean the external guns and the associated gear with high-pressure air and cleaning solvent. Also, all the helicopter bases had metal flight decks for this exact reason: to keep the sand out of the engines, and the various ball bearings, and as in the above episode with the external guns. But after that and other episodes, at every opportunity if I had time, I always grabbed the head of each rocket in the pod and gave a little yank and twist to see it was loose and hopefully good to go when fired.

Early in the year 1967, while still getting my feet wet as a gunner, our normal missions involved escorting the transport choppers on resupply at remote Marine outposts, medevac escorts, insertions/extractions of Recon teams, and so on. But shortly after I started flying, we were dispatched on a mission about 20 klicks southwest of Chu Lai looking for VC who had been sniping at a Marine grunt patrol. We had been flying low to the ground searching for the enemy snipers when we finally caught several VC on the run, trying to get away back into the foothills and under cover. I was in the lead bird and the pilot was really making that Huey dance, doing figure eights, up, down, circling back and forth chasing the VC. However, and unfortunately for me, I wasn't much help on that mission; my "gourmet" breakfast that morning had been too much greasy canned bacon and powdered eggs, along with the "whole grain" toast, because I spent most of the mission, or I should say "ordeal," with my head stuck out the open door regurgitating all over the southern portion of the I Corps area. Whether or not the rest of the flight crew noticed, I don't know, but as we were flying back to Ky Ha, I worried that I wasn't going to be able to fly because of airsickness; but nobody said anything and I survived, said nothing and kept it to myself. But that was the only time I got airsick in Nam.

While in Vietnam I, as well as the other flight crews, was able to see just about every square mile of South Vietnam's I Corps area, and then some. After I started flying one of the most important things I did was to buy a Pentax 35mm camera. I kept the camera in the helicopter under my seat all the time. During the nighttime hours, the ordnance guys would come around to clean the exterior guns, change parts, or whatever. Every morning when I got up to inspect the bird, the camera was always right there under my seat; no one ever bothered with it, no matter where we might have to stop for the night.

At Ky Ha, there was a small PX and whenever I needed, I would buy two or three rolls of 36 exposure 35mm color slides, and as soon

TIME TO START FLYING • 47

Posing by our Huey.

LCpl Pete Harris.

LCpl Ferrera.

as I used up the film, I would mail them home. When I got home in February 1968, I was surprised to discover that I had taken almost 1,500 photos, which obviously I had never seen before. Most of them were aerial views from just about everywhere in the I Corps area, but some of them were redundant, and many were out of focus; it wasn't easy trying to capture many of the scenes that I wanted to take, especially when we were low to the ground with the VC waiting for an opportunity to shoot us down. There was little time to grab the camera and take a picture when the opportunity presented itself, but nevertheless, it also exposed my amateurish photography skills.

Unfortunately, later in the fall, shortly after the squadron moved to Quang Tri, we had been sent out aboard a helicopter carrier for two days and had to spend the night aboard the ship. That night while I was taking a shower with obviously very little privacy for anyone in the shower room, somehow an asshole "squid" took off with my watch and wallet. The next morning while inspecting the bird I also discovered that my camera with two or three rolls of exposed film had also been stolen. For an entire year in Nam, no one, not one of the Marines touched my camera but one night on a navy ship, some asshole took all my personal stuff.

Several days prior to the theft of my camera, late one night the NVA and Viet Cong had tried to overrun Camp Evans, the Marine base camp just a few miles southwest of the air base at Quang Tri. We were sent down to that area the next morning on another mission, and as we passed over the camp, I took several photos of the pile of the VC/NVA bodies that had been killed along the perimeter. I have often wondered if the Good Lord above did not approve of me taking those photos, then possibly showing pictures of those dead bodies. Those photos were on the rolls of exposed film in the camera, or attached to the camera strap, and perhaps that was the reason I lost my camera.

I was without a camera for several weeks, but eventually, we were called for missions in the Da Nang area working with the Marine Recon teams in that area. Luckily that Recon base camp was located very close to the big Post Exchange at Freedom Hill at Da Nang, and whenever we got the opportunity to work in that area, we would ask permission to stop, and I was able to buy another camera.

At any rate, I took photos of every Marine camp and outpost in the I Corps area at every opportunity when possible, and not being shot at, of course. One big regret was that I hadn't taken more photos of the guys in the squadron, especially the pilots and other crew chiefs, whom I had flown with hundreds of times. The fact was that if his bird was "up" and available, a crew chief would be flying just about every day, and were always heading in different directions on day standby. Later in the day when we finally returned from the various away assignments, there was limited time together back at Ky Ha or Quang Tri, and generally socializing was mostly limited to the guys in our own section and hooch. At times, as for the crew chiefs, we probably spent more time with the pilots when we were away at outlying assignments, and regrettably I didn't have the foresight to take photos of many of the pilots that I worked with on a given day.

I've seen several reports that a total of about three million military personnel served in Vietnam during the war; but also, only one in five (20 percent) who were there actually pulled a trigger in combat. The war was very different for a lot of people depending on where they were located, and what their MOS was. I can say with absolute certainty that those who flew in helicopters pulled the trigger thousands of times, and probably more than anybody else, even the grunts; and it didn't matter which type of helicopter they flew in.

That said, there were definite advantages to those of us who were in helicopters; for the most part, we slept on a cot or bed just about every night, were able to take a shower on most nights, and much of the time we had a mess hall with hot meals. We didn't have to sleep in fox holes for nights on end, didn't have to deal with the bugs, the snakes, or the leeches, nor had clothes rot off our back, or jungle rot on our feet. Or had to wonder if that noise you just heard, in the middle of night in the dark while you were in a fox hole, was real or not. Could it be the VC, or the NVA? The grunts and the Marine Recon had all that and more. The only thing that everyone had to get used to, on the ground, or anywhere near the remote areas of I Corps, was the mosquitoes at night. We had a choice: try to sleep in mosquito netting and sweat like crazy in the heat and humidity, or listen to those little bastards buzzing in your ear. It took me a while to get used to that, but eventually, most everyone did. I can't even imagine how the grunts and the Recon guys handled it out in the bush.

I'm certain that most of the Marines in I Corps were not in that 80 percent who didn't fire a bullet while in Nam. I consider myself to have been very, very fortunate, like the other flight crews in not only VMO-6, but all those in the helicopter community in the I Corps area: we had the unique opportunity that we were able to sit back and see just about every aspect of the Vietnam War in our area.

CHAPTER 7

Land Shark

"Land Shark" was the Military Operations Agency which controlled all aircraft in the I Corps area of South Vietnam. We received our orders/missions either directly or indirectly from Land Shark.

A week or so later, after a mission, we were returning to Ky Ha after inserting a Marine Recon team in the foothills and mountains southwest of Chu Lai, when Land Shark called with another mission. On that day we had been the lead gunship, and Land Shark gave my pilot a Marine unit's call sign and their radio frequency, and indicated they might be in trouble, and directed us to head north up toward the foothills southwest of the town of Tam Ky. The Marine unit turned out to be a small truck convoy of grunts who were trying to get back to their base camp.

Flying north we could see black smoke in the distance, in the general area of where the Marines were supposed to be. The pilot was able to contact the Marine unit and told the officer in charge that we were a section of gunships and would be flying in from the south, their "six o'clock" position, and asked for their "sitrep" (situation report). The convoy officer said that they were a platoon of grunts in two or three 6x6 military trucks and that they had stopped short of a small village on the dirt road leading back to their base camp, but that there was good size fire coming from within the village, and it looked suspicious. He also reported that he had sent about a dozen Marines out in different directions into the surrounding rice paddies to form a temporary perimeter, and that we should watch out for them. We were still several klicks out when both gunships dropped down to treetop level so that if there were

VC present and/or planning anything, they would not hear us coming. My pilot then radioed to the chase bird that when we arrived over the convoy, we were going to break to the right, and for them to go left, so that we could immediately start checking out the areas on both sides of the Marines on the ground.

Several minutes later we zoomed in just over the Marines' heads flying at about 120 knots. We swung off to the right which put me on the east side of the convoy; the chase bird went left. As we flew by, when the Marines in the trucks realized that Marine gunships had arrived, providing them overhead protection, they all started jumping and cheering, giving us the thumbs up. It was then, at that very moment that it struck me, and I knew that I had one of the best jobs in the Vietnam War. I will never forget that moment, and those grunts who were so excited to see Marine Huey gunships overhead and watching over them.

Like most FNGs in early 1967, I was not that far removed from that young boy, who just eight or 10 years ago used to watch *Mighty Mouse* on the black-and-white TV with my younger brothers, with its theme song, "Here I come to Save the Day"; and for a moment or two, I pictured myself as the hero, just like Mighty Mouse. I'm an old man now, but that fantasy is still alive in my head. My wife happened to see this quote, which was made by an anonymous USMC general, and she cut it out of the VFW magazine she was reading and pasted it on one of the pictures above my head: "There is nothing like the sound of a Huey coming over the mountains."

As we were flying around, surveying the village and surrounding area, it was apparent that those grunts were indeed in a very precarious and potentially dangerous situation; there was no doubt that there were plenty of Viet Cong in the area, who were possibly getting ready to attack the grunts' vulnerability. There were 40–50 Marines gathered in two or three military trucks sitting there, caught out in the open with nowhere to go for cover.

As we rotated around the trucks for several more minutes checking out the village and surrounding area, there was no sign of enemy activity that we could see. Whether or not the VC were there, but went into hiding, we'll never know. When the chase pilot reported that they also saw no sign of enemy activity, then my pilot radioed to the ground unit that everything appeared to be normal. And with that, the grunt CO called in his perimeter guard and after several more minutes, they proceeded on their way. We flew "shotgun" over them while they motored through the village, and for a short distance further, then headed back to Ky Ha for our next mission. But during that early mission, and that sequence of events, which I think about often, I will never forget the excitement, the exhilaration that I felt that day; indeed, I had one of the best jobs in the Vietnam War.

I learned very quickly that when the action started there was no idle time; everyone on the bird had something to do. The two of us sitting behind were busy protecting our side of the bird and keeping those six machine guns working. Each of the six M-60s had a cyclic rate of fire of about 500 rounds per minute (or 3,000 rounds a minute), and when things got "hot," so did those machine gun barrels, and believe me the guns jammed frequently. After a couple minutes of steady firing the heat would cause the barrel to swell, and when they got too hot, the bullet extractor would rip off the end of the round, leaving the brass casing behind, causing the gun to jam.

Besides the barrels getting hot and jamming, another common reason for most of the external gun jams was a "long round," which occurred when the belts of 7.62 bullets were moving from the ammo boxes below our seats through the flexible metal guides which fed the external machine guns. If one of those bullets in the belt was not fully seated, and protruding even slightly forward from the rest of the rounds, it would cause a jam. The two most important duties of the two guys behind the pilots were to keep those four exterior machine guns and their door guns firing; and, of course, to keep the bad guys on your side of the bird from shooting you down. As soon as the situation permitted, we would have to scurry to find the cause of the jam and get those feed belts hooked back up to the outside machine gun. There wasn't any time to fool around; keep those guns working and get back on your door gun and protect your side of the bird. And as soon as possible, clean those gun barrels. The Viet Cong and the North Vietnamese were always shooting at the helicopters, and up there in the Vietnam sky there were no fox holes to jump into, nor a big boulder or tree to hide behind; there was nowhere to hide, period. The fact was that shooting back was really our only means of defense. It wasn't very long before us NFG's were no longer gunners; the squadron moved us over to the left side and gave us our own birds, and that was when I oversaw my bird and I always had two extra gun barrels on the floor in front of us, among other weapons.

Except for the flight crew's body protection, just about everything on a helicopter is made of lightweight materials, and all the helicopter's functioning parts have no or minimal protection against enemy gunfire. On the UH-1E, as well as the other choppers, efforts were made to protect the flight crews; each pilot up front was sitting on a roughly half-inch bulletproof board under his seat and behind his back, and alongside both seats were 10-inch vertical side plates up to their shoulders made of the same material. But other than their flak jackets and "bullet bouncers" on their chests, most everything in front of them was plexiglass. The crew chief and gunner sat on the same material as the pilots to somewhat protect from enemy fire, but there wasn't much more that was feasible for providing protection for the two of us in the back during a firefight: we were both constantly moving around. But both of us wore safety belts, with a 4-feet lead, so that we didn't fall out during "intense" flight. The engine, the transmission, and the driveshaft were basically unprotected; only the lightweight aircraft cowlings covered them. Initially, the flight crews wore just flak jackets, which were not much good against enemy bullets, but several months after I arrived, they came out with the "bullet bouncers," both front and back, and made of the same material as the seats; they were heavy, but they worked; and would stop a .50 caliber bullet.

Later in the day or at night, when the birds had returned and were finished for the day, the ordnance guys would drive around with their tractor and wagon load of supplies to the gunships, and they would give the external guns a thorough cleaning with cleaning solutions and pressurized air; then they would refill the external ammo boxes under the back seats, and refill the ammo tray on the floor behind the pilots with two dozen 100-round boxes of 7.62 for the door guns. As I recall, we generally carried about 10–12,000 rounds of 7.62 ammo for machine guns, with rockets, and there were many times when I wondered if the pilot was going to be able to get us airborne with that much weight aboard.

The USMC, being part of the US navy, apparently played second fiddle with the funding for helicopter replacement parts, and thus we heard numerous times, "The Marines do more with less." But why the military supply system during Nam was not fully funded, I'm not sure; however, there has been much written and reported about corruption during the war, and probably all wars. No doubt VMOs 2 and 3, and the other USMC squadrons, had the same problem procuring spare helicopter parts. Thankfully, we always had sufficient ammo available. But I remember that VMO-6, while still at Ky Ha, every week or two, would send a Huey slick with a couple of senior NCOs down the big US Army helicopter base just below the Quang Ngai in II Corps' area to barter and swap captured enemy items for replacement parts to keep our birds flying. It was a common occurrence at Ky Ha during our time there. Generally, on those trips the "heavies" were also able to bring back several cases of Budweiser for the squadron, but it was warm Budweiser.

Compared to the US Army with its huge fleet of helicopters, I believe that the helicopter squadrons of the Marine Air Wing were much smaller in size, and in personnel. I am guesstimating, but I would say the average monthly population of VMO-6 was about 150 Marines, made up of the different specialties. Our MOSs were pilots, crew chiefs, ordnance, tinsmiths, clerical and supply, etc., with squadron personnel coming and going all the time. Each of us had different rotation dates during our 13-month tours; there were new faces all the time, and then suddenly the "old salts," like Sergeant Johnson, my first crew chief, rotated home.

The distance from Highway One at Dong Ha to Khe Sanh by road was about 30–35 miles, then the road continued into Laos.

They reiterated that the missions were classified, and that we were strictly prohibited from reporting any information, or observations, of the missions to the outside world, or even to the rest of the squadron when we returned to Ky Ha. Basically, our missions would be very much the same as working with Marine Recon, to escort and protect the South Vietnamese CH-34 transport helicopters during insertions and extractions and support the SF advisors and their SOG teams while they were on the ground.

The first thing the next morning, before we departed the Special Forces Camp for Khe Sanh, they took all our personal identification, but gave back these items later that day when we returned to the SF camp at Phu Bai. (I don't recall them taking our IDs after that initial day.) They also gave each of the crew chiefs a can of green spray paint and instructed them to paint over the "US Marines" and any markings on the tail booms of our gunships. Of course, my crew chief handed the can of paint to me and it ended up being my job. And lastly and most importantly, they also indicated that in the event any of us were shot down, that they would do everything possible to get us out. But they also stressed that the reason there were eight helicopters and the main reason for four gunships was to better protect the transport choppers during insertion and extractions and while the team was on the ground; bottom line, we would have to take care of ourselves if one of us was shot down. But if anyone did get shot down and no rescue could be made, our best chance of survival would be to head as far west as we could into Laos and hope to find "friendlies" there; meaning, we would be on our own.

The next morning after that the last briefing we departed for Khe Sanh; it would be the first time that I went there, but certainly not the last. The SOG missions at Khe Sanh lasted through to September 1967, and we operated out of Khe Sanh probably two to three days a week during that time. When we returned to Ky Ha after the initial SOG missions a couple days later, those of us who frequented those SOG missions decided to bring along our own personal long weapons;

I checked out an M-16 from the ordnance department and it stayed in my bird the rest of my tour.

Only a week or so later, even though I didn't think that I was ready or qualified, the squadron moved me to the left side of the bird as a "provisional" crew chief, and I was assigned my own bird (WB#7). I believe that it was the same scenario for Pete Harris; he also moved over and was given his own bird (WB #20). It was then that I decided that my bird would routinely carry an M-79 grenade launcher, and at least one case of 40mm grenades, plus several hand fragmentation grenades, which I wrapped in duct tape, and I stashed them in the side compartment on my side of the bird. Along with my M-16 with two magazines, these stayed in my birds for the rest of my tour.

Shortly after I was assigned my first bird, one bright and sunny day I was out on the top of the bird inspecting the rotor head and its various parts on the daily pre-flight inspection. The swashplate on a UH-1E Huey is a round lightweight solid metal apparatus about two feet in diameter that encircles the "mast," a metal pipe that extends upward from the transmission to the rotor head. The swashplate has three outward extensions molded of the same material, and each of the extensions has about a three-quarter-inch divide at the end where the control rod bearings from the pilot's controls are attached. Those rods control the helicopter's rotor head, with up and down, and right and left movements. In the bright sunlight, I noticed that two of the three swashplate extensions had tiny hairline cracks where the bearings on the control rods hook on.

I immediately went to find my section leader, Sergeant Sherrill, and happened to come across Staff Sergeant Whitham, who was the squadron's Quality Control NCO. Then I found and alerted Sergeant Sherrill and told them that they better come look at the swashplate on my bird. I distinctly remember Staff Sergeant Whitham's reaction when he saw the cracks: "Holy shit!" It would be only a matter of time before one or both control rods became detached from the swashplate, and then the pilot would have lost control of the helicopter, and we would have fallen out of the sky. The reason for the two cracks is anyone's guess; it could have been over-torquing the nuts and bolts, but my guess, it was probably just the severe stress that the UH-1E Huey had to endure in Vietnam during fire fights.

Fortunately, the Bell Helicopters representative, who was regularly visiting the VMO squadrons, happened to be at Ky Ha that day. He was also shocked to see the cracks. We obviously had to replace the damaged swashplate with a new one. And in quick order, only a couple days later, Bell quickly came out with reinforcing plates, to be added on each side of the swashplate extensions, along with longer bolts that had to be installed on all the other UH-1E Hueys. But again, I was lucky to have found those cracks before something bad happened; and it was the first of several times that I was lucky in Nam, those events to be reported later. I have to believe that I must have been in good graces with the Lord.

Oftentimes I've thought that when they invented the helicopter, would they have had any idea what the Vietnam War would demand of those helicopters? The amount of stress on those rotor heads and controls that was necessary to operate in the Vietnam war zone was extraordinary. Initially, I don't think that they foresaw the effect that Vietnam's weather would have on how the helicopter had to be operated daily in Nam. Everything was made of lightweight material, almost always had overload/weight limitations on takeoff, and the acrobatic maneuvers needed almost all the time. And I think now, 50-plus years later, that I maintained and repaired my helicopters numerous times, and I'm still here writing this book. I have been blessed.

The SOG missions were not everyday assignments but called as needed by MACV. On those days when we were to be assigned to the SOG missions generally we would find out the night before, or when we reported to the flight hooch early that the morning; they were on the flight schedule as SOG TAD (temporary assigned duty), and as I remember we would be 4-1, 4-2, 4-3 and 4-4. As I recall, my bird was always 4-1, most likely because I was in section 1 and VMO-6 section 1 birds were WB#1 thru 7.

Generally, we were not away from the squadron for more than two or three days at a time. I'm not sure if it was always the same squadron personnel necessarily, but because of the classified status, I think that they tried to minimize the number of people involved with those

SOG missions. Although I'm certain that the crew chiefs (Corporals Harris, Schneider, Evans, and myself) had a steady diet of SOG missions through the summer. The SOG missions were not on a set schedule, maybe once or twice a week, and on the off days we would be intermingled with other regular assignments back at Ky Ha. I don't remember for the most part who the pilots or the gunners might have been. But that was also true regarding almost all missions that I had throughout my tour. However, I remember it was primarily the same crew chiefs on the SOG missions; not necessarily the same pilots, nor the gunners who took turns as the gunners during different months for normal missions.

When MACV-SOG notified the squadron and scheduled missions, the four gunships would fly to the Phu Bai SF camp first thing in the morning. I don't remember having any social contact with the South Vietnamese CH-34 pilots, nor with the mercenary teams that the SF employed. Nor am I sure where they would stay before and after the missions, but most likely most of the SF teams on the ground during those missions were locals from the Montagnard village nearby Khe Sanh.

"Montagnard" is a French term meaning "mountain people," and they mostly lived in the highlands and mountains of Vietnam. The SF guys at Phu Bai said that they also had hired some Chinese Nung. The foreign mercenaries no doubt stayed at the SF camp at Phu Bai, because of racial animosity, which the SF guys at their camp at Phu Bai said was prevalent in Nam, and I suspect that some of the Montagnard on those SOG missions could have been from further south. The SF also had their own compound at Lang Vei, which was near Montagnard village. There were always a few local Montagnard at Khe Sanh who helped us with rearming the birds when the SOG teams were on the ground. I'm pretty sure that most of the SF team were inhabitants of the Montagnard village, which was several miles west of Khe Sanh, but we had no contact with the hired guns who were also used on the SOG missions.

But the fact was that the Vietnamese, the Montagnard, and the Chinese did not like each other. The SF base camp at Phu Bai was adjacent to the South Vietnamese boot camp/ training facility; there was only concertina wire separating the two entities. The SF guys told us to be cautious walking around the areas separating their camp and the Vietnamese, because it was not uncommon for a firefight to break out among the foreign mercenaries. I can only imagine the problems that the SF team leaders must have had on the ground in "no man's land" with those hired guns grimacing at each other. We did not have any close contact with the mercenaries, or the SF advisors in the field while on the SOG missions; the only opportunity to socialize with the SF soldiers was back at their camp at Phu Bai.

One night Pete Harris and I were sitting in the SF bar/ hooch, which served as their camp club. We were drinking Russian cognac. Suddenly a grenade exploded right outside the club. Both Harris and I drew our handguns, wondering what had happened. We looked over our shoulders at the SF bartender who had picked up his M-16 and had it pointed at the door, which was the only entrance to the hooch, while the three of us waited for someone to come charging through the door, or for something to happen. Finally, after a few minutes, the bartender relaxed, put down his M-16, and said that it happened every now and then: an RVN soldier would throw a grenade, or shoot at one of the mercenaries; but that was the extent of that episode.

I recall that during our time on the SOG missions, the Vietnamese CH-34s, did, in fact, have their share of battle damage, but fortunately we did not lose any while we were escorting them. However, there was one advantage that we enjoyed while staying over at the SF camp, the beer was cold and the drinks were dirt cheap, and it was the first time I had ever tasted cognac. Back at Ky Ha, we were lucky to get a couple of cans of warm Budweiser once every two to three weeks.

Early in the mornings of the SOG missions, we gunships would always fly north separately and then rendezvous with the Vietnamese CH-34s and the teams at Khe Sanh, and as soon as everybody was ready, we would take off for parts mostly west and south of Khe Sanh. I don't remember not being Klondike (our squadron's call sign) 4-1 while on the SOG missions, and my pilot was generally in charge of the SOG operation during flight; he was frequently communicating with the SF SOG team leader until insertion at the landing zone (LZ). Once the team was safely on the ground the 34s would return to Khe Sanh and wait there until the extraction time. Depending on the mission, the gunships would stay overhead in another area, so as not to expose the team's location, or return to Khe Sanh for refueling and/or rearming if necessary.

Every mission seemed to be different, and the SF command was not interested in letting us know about the nature of a given mission. We were there to protect the transport choppers in flight and support the team while on the ground. (Later in life I came to understand that if we had been shot down and captured, we would not have been able to divulge anything if we didn't know why we were there.) SOG missions were basically much the same as working with Marine Recon teams, especially in the Khe Sanh area. We weren't told anything about the Marine Recon missions either. Those missions were maybe six to eight Marines, while the SOG teams were much larger, perhaps 20–25 hired guns with their SF team leaders, but the insertion and extraction procedures were basically the same; other than the fact on SOG missions we were somewhere we weren't supposed to be.

The only good memory I have of the SOG missions was the first one, four gunships and four Vietnamese CH-34s, which we referred to as the "King Bees." (The US must have given the South Vietnamese some old CH-34s after which they painted them all black with big yellow eyes; they looked like, and we called them, bees.) On the first mission we departed Khe Sanh and flew a good distance northwest, obviously well into Laos, to an area where the foothills and mountains flatten out into a wide-open valley. It was there where the SF teams found what they were looking for that day; evidence of the North Vietnamese truck traffic, lots of heavy truck tire impressions on the ground. I remember the SOG team's radio chatter about making "plaster of Paris" impressions, to prove to Congress that North Vietnam was sending supplies south. If there were any NVA in the area, then they stayed out of sight, because I don't recall having contact with them that first day. After that mission it was a good bet that on subsequent insertions when and if they discovered any NVA trucks they would destroy them, ambush and capture NVA when given the chance. They were operating covertly and what they were doing was classified. I have no idea at what point the NVA had to stop using trucks for the transportation of war supplies, as most of the Ho Chi Minh Trail was nothing but mountains, hills and very thick jungle.

But during the rest of my tour, especially with Marine Recon, numerous times we spotted a few elephants here and there, and water buffalo, which were their main means of moving those supplies.

During the SOG missions, after we arrived at Khe Sanh, there were several times when the "King Bees" were "no shows" for whatever reason, but I suspect that the CH-34s were older versions and probably mechanical issues might have been the reason. Or, that day's mission might have been suddenly cancelled. At any rate, the reason for cancellation was not for us to know. Whenever there were "no shows," generally SOG would hand us back over to Marine Operations for the day. There were several of the SOG missions where we had additional missions for the following day(s), but we would generally return to the SF camp at Phu Bai for the night. However, if the team was still on the ground at the end of that day, they would keep us at Khe Sanh for the night. They did this only when necessary as they didn't like keeping helicopters at Khe Sanh overnight because of NVA mortar and artillery fire. But when returning to the SF camp for the night, which we enjoyed, we were able to socialize with the SF advisors and enjoy the refreshments at their club.

There was one thing that at first really surprised me, and somewhat was concerning and made me curious: it was the security of our gunships when we stayed overnight at the SF camp. I'm not sure where the RVN 34s stayed, or where they put up for the night; the only time we would see the 34s was at Khe Sanh. Most probably the "King Bees" stayed at the Vietnamese side of the Phu Bai Air Base, or at the RVN boot camp/training facility, but I'm not sure. But our gunships were parked for the night right across the road from the entrance of the SF camp on Highway One with civilian traffic coming and going all the time. It just seemed to me that the birds were very vulnerable overnight when we stayed there; however, during the six months of "off and on" missions that we worked for SOG, nothing ever happened. I can only surmise that local traffic must have been suspended after certain hours, and/or security beefed up around the birds; but at any rate, every morning when it was time to saddle up for the missions, the birds were always there, good to go.

At the SF camp at Phu Bai about a quarter mile north on Highway One there was an orphanage, a South Vietnamese Catholic orphanage,

One of my favorite pictures from Nam, with local kids.

I believe. I walked up there a couple of times with my camera and took photos of the little kids. Several times some of the boys would run down to the birds whenever they saw us waiting for the pilots and getting ready to take off. We used to share with them some of the contents of our C-Rations. We've all heard tales of the Viet Cong using little kids to hide explosives on them to kill Americans, but whether or not any of that was true or not is anybody's guess; those little guys were just like any other normal kids. One of the photos that I took with them was next to my bird, four little guys, perhaps 8–10 years old; it is one of my favorite pictures that I took in Nam.

Later in life, looking at that photo, the sad reality occurred to me that I took that picture in early summer of 1967 and that the war would continue for eight more years, and I wondered if any of the four little guys had survived. During those days in Vietnam, as soon as young boys reached their teenage years, or became of military age, and those little guys would have, they would either end up in the RVN military, or with the Viet Cong. In the I Corps area that I saw, there were no civilian teenage boys during the war; only young kids, old men, and old women, and no one "in between."

CHAPTER 9

The Hill Battles at Khe Sanh

One day, early in April 1967, while working SOG missions at Khe Sanh, we were awaiting the arrival of the SOG teams and the "King Bees." While sitting there alongside the northwest end of the airstrip, I noticed that a Marine patrol was moving out through the wire at the north perimeter and moving up toward Hill 861. I grabbed my camera and ran closer to take a photo of the grunts heading out; later that day, a couple hours after they had left Khe Sanh, we learned that the patrol had run into a North Vietnamese ambush on the hills overlooking Khe Sanh. Unfortunately, we were of no help to those Marines as we were in the middle of a SOG mission, waiting for them to call for extraction.

But that morning turned out to be the first day of the battle for Hills 861 and 881 which would be famously known as the "Hill Battles" at Khe Sanh. For the next several days, while we continued to work the SOG missions, I was able to take photos of the battle while we were refueling/rearming at Khe Sanh. During that week and the start of the Hill Battles, several times as we were flying by Hill 861 on the way to the SOG mission area, the NVA would take pot-shots at us as we flew by. I replied with two or three M-79 grenades on the top of the hill. I have no idea if I hit anything.

During the Hill Battles, while we were at Khe Sanh on SOG missions, Land Shark had other sections of Marine gunships and CH-46 choppers there as well (most probably the gunships from VMO-3 out of Phu Bai, as well as the 46s), who were supporting the grunts who were fighting their way up Hills 861 and 881. There were several occasions when I was able to take photos of the other Hueys and the 46s in action, as we were watching the air strikes while we were refueling/rearming on the SOG missions. We had a clear view of the fighting on Hill 861, which was less than a mile away. Khe Sanh was virtually surrounded by higher terrain and mountains and no doubt the NVA had had it under constant surveillance. Later in the year the artillery or mortar rounds would fall whenever supply aircraft arrived. We soon concluded that the NVA had located spotters on the higher mountain peaks overlooking the Khe Sanh area, along the Ho Chi Minh Trail, and in the DMZ there, to alert them of the SOG teams and Marine Recon insertions.

Speaking of lookout positions, shortly after the squadron started working the SOG missions, after completing our SOG missions for the day there were several times when Land Shark had us escort Marine CH-34s on resupply runs. The location of the resupply was a very remote outpost that we referred to as the "Tiger's Tooth." (I've seen in print that there was a Tiger Mountain in the Khe Sanh area, but if they are one and the same, I don't know.) The Tiger's Tooth outpost was about two miles directly north of Khe Sanh, in an extremely remote mountainous area; it was either a Marine or a Special Forces observation post and very small. I do not recall what its actual military designated name was, but from the air, it looked like a tiger's canine tooth. The north side of the outpost was straight up and down, about a 500-foot-plus drop. The south side appeared to be at least a 50- to 60-degree incline up to the outpost. It was only inhabited by a very small number of Marines or SF, or perhaps Marine Recon, but a guesstimate of 15–20 Marines or SF manned the outpost. Certainly not a lot of people, especially when they were surrounded by NVA in the area. The thing I remember most about the two to three resupplies that I was involved with was that the most urgent request was for more cigarettes. Those poor guys manning that outpost must have been basket cases. Such a small number surrounded by the NVA, half the time in fog or cloud cover, and especially when night came, and with no immediate help nearby. I believe that the MACV must have decided to abandon Tiger's Tooth not long after our last resupply mission. In my opinion, the outpost was untenable.

After several SOG missions, it became apparent to the squadron flight crews that the situation was entirely different from those routine missions out of Ky Ha. Working on the SOG missions off and on for the first half of my tour, and later in the year with Marine Recon teams up around the DMZ and the Khe Sanh region, there was no immediate backup nearby in the event one of us had been shot down. Conversely, while working missions in the southern I Corps area, the squadron had extra gunships nearby at Ky Ha that could easily be scrambled, and within the hour there would be help overhead if needed, and plus more refueling and rearming facilities in the area. But that was not the case at Khe Sanh, especially the rearming aspect there. Other than a couple of the locals from the Montagnard village, there was very little logistical help at Khe Sanh. It was all hands on deck reloading ammunition and rockets, and it was more time consuming, especially when the SOG or the Recon team was in trouble.

Most of the 2.75-inch rockets that we used on the gunships at Khe Sanh were transported and stored in wood crates, and as I recall, there were four rockets in each wooden crate. For safety purposes, each of the rockets had a very heavy gauge wire tightly secured around the metal side near the end of the propellant end of the rocket with the opposite end of the wire bent around and making secure contact on the 1-inch diameter ignition button. The wire was there to prevent static electricity from accidentally igniting the rocket. Without the proper tool and care for pulling off the wire, it was more time consuming, and it was easy to accidentally cut yourself; I know, I ripped my skin on my little finger one day while we were hurrying to get back in the air because a SOG or a Recon team was in trouble. I recall that at the three VMO bases, the Ordnance guys always took care of keeping an adequate number of rockets available to go for the gunships which were in dire need to get in the air. They took care of removing the rockets from the crates and taking the wires off the rockets, getting them ready. They had dozens of them stored in a non-metallic container on their wagon that they hauled around to quickly reload the rocket pods, as well as plenty of 7.62 ammo for the external machine guns; but that was not the case at Khe Sanh. At Khe Sanh, especially on the SOG missions, with the team on the ground and in contact with the NVA, and four gunships on a "hot" refuel and rearm, there might have been a couple dozen rockets ready to go, but not the 56 rockets that we needed when there were four of us.

CHAPTER 10

CH-46 Downed

While working the SOG missions, occasionally MACV would turn us back over to Land Shark's control and Marine operations/missions, which were more than happy to have four gunships available. On one such occasion, with the SOG missions cancelled, Land Shark assigned us to escort two Marine Recon insert missions. We were working with two CH-46s, each transporting a Marine Recon team with two different LZ locations; one landing zone was north and the other one south of Khe Sanh.

On the first Recon team insertion, we took off (four gunships and two 46s) and flew for about 10 minutes northeast from Khe Sanh, which was clearly on the northern edge of the DMZ. (Unlike the area east near the South China Sea, in the far western end of the DMZ in the mountains, there was no indication where the North and South started or ended; it was nothing but jungle.)

We arrived at the designated landing zone (LZ) for the first team, which was mostly hills and mountains amid heavy vegetation, but their LZ was a small grassy area just large enough for a CH-46 to land. I have no clue if the landing zone was still in South Vietnam. The pilot instructed both 46s to stay off in the distance while we dropped down to check out the LZ area, and then informed our chase gunships that we would be going in from the south to north, turning back around to the west and would cover 4-4 as they pulled out of the zone. We flew in first at treetop level, with 4-2, 4-3, and 4-4 following, rotating around while covering each other's six o'clock. Everything was quiet, no sign of the NVA, no fire; then the pilot radioed the 46 with the first team aboard to fall in behind the second gunship, and 4-3 and 4-4 would follow him. The CH-46 fell in behind 4-2 and landed; all went well, no fireworks. We hung around the area for a few minutes and then when the first Recon team called "clear" and reported that they were OK, we departed the area and headed southwest of Khe Sanh for the second drop zone.

Flying about the same distance south of Khe Sanh we located the second LZ, maybe 10–12 klicks from Khe Sanh. This landing zone was on the south side of a good-size hill and was covered with tall elephant grass. At the top of the hill there was a ridgeline; beyond the ridgeline was covered with heavy foliage and jungle. Again, the pilot radioed both 46s to stay off in the distance while we checked out this LZ; it would be the same procedure as the first insert. We did the same routine except we would be flying east to west, then rotating back around to the south, to cover 4-4 when they pulled out. Again, we swooped down to treetop level followed by the three chase birds; although we did not receive any fire, there looked to be a freshly dug trench line along the top of the hill at the edge of the jungle.

After our first pass over the top of the hill, we rotated back around to recheck the top of the hill again while the chase birds followed, circling back over the bottom of the hill. As we were again flying over the crest of the hill, one of the chase pilots came on the radio to report that his crew chief had spotted something on the lower part of the hill. I believe that it was the crew chief in 4-3, Corporal Evans, who spotted what appeared to be a tunnel opening toward the bottom of the hill. With the evidence of NVA activity on the top of the hill and then the discovery of the tunnel entrance toward the bottom, the pilot called the second Recon team leader, who I believe was a young lieutenant, and suggested that we should find another drop zone because this place looked very suspicious.

After a few more minutes, with apparently no available or suitable LZs in the nearby area, the team leader declined, and decided that we needed to keep the original LZ. Whether the Recon team leader had consulted with his Recon Operations Group with his own radio is anyone's guess, but the fact was that all four gunships had flown very low over the top of the hill without enemy fire. Now, many years later, I can only surmise what my pilot must have been thinking. As far as we could see there was nothing but mountains and jungle; there was not a more favorable LZ in sight, and none of us had taken any fire. With time becoming a factor, the pilot decided he didn't have a choice and ceded to the team leader's opinion. With the decision made, he then instructed the second 46 with team 2 aboard, that we would do the same procedure as the first: the second 46 would follow behind 4-2, followed by 4-3 and 4-4.

We again led the flight in at treetop level directly above the top of the hill and 4-2 followed. But because of the gradient on the slope with the trees and jungle on top of the hill, the 46 had to veer off to the left and land slightly downhill, perhaps 30 yards or so from the crest. The pilot on the 46 had to touch down on only his rear right wheel, and hover on his right side to remain level. As he was settling down on the side of the hill, he was followed by 4-3 and 4-4. We were rotating back around directly to the south of the hovering 46 in the LZ, I was looking at the 46 from my side of the bird, and as we watched him come to a hover, suddenly the jungle on top of the hill came alive with muzzle flashes as the NVA opened fire on the 46. Immediately, the 46 was down and started rolling over on its side with its rotor blades digging into the downhill slope of the hill, breaking off, and flying off in different directions. I remember the 46 rolled over once and down the hill a bit further, and immediately started on fire. It came to rest on its left side. Obviously, the NVA were waiting for the bigger target, the CH-46 and more people aboard, and let us gunships pass by; but it could have been any one of us, we were so very fortunate.

All four gunships started blasting away, but for me and the other crew chiefs, rotating around and looking from south to north, the downed 46 was so close to the top of the hill where the NVA fire was coming from that it was very difficult to fire over the top of the 46 and into the jungle; it was so close and dangerous, trying to control our fire over the downed crew and at the NVA. Whether there also were NVA hiding below the downed 46 in the elephant grass, I don't know, but we kept a perimeter of fire all around the burning 46.

After a few minutes, we started to see the Marines crawling out the back of the chopper and helping each other. Fortunately, with the 46 on its side and with the rear ramp down, it offered some concealment and helped protect them from further NVA fire as they were struggling out of the bird. After a few minutes, they finally were out and were huddled on the downhill side of the burning chopper as we continued to blast away at the NVA.

As we were strafing east to west on top of the hill, at the end of our gun run and directly above the top of the hill, that put the 46 and downed crew on my side which limited my firing range as I could not fire my M-60 straight down because of the exterior guns and the rocket pods; so I decided to use the three hand grenades I had stashed away in the bird because the NVA were directly below us. The next time around I pulled off the tape and the pin and threw it straight down, but because of our air speed and the grenade's momentum, I watched it bounce harmlessly away in the jungle and west of the trench. The second time around I pulled the pin, counted to two seconds, and dropped it out, trying to get it to explode directly above the trench-line which it did. But 4-2, covering behind us, came on the radio and said "4-1, I just saw an airburst behind you." I immediately told the pilot that it was me, and I had thrown a fragmentation grenade. The pilot then informed the chase birds that it wasn't anti-air fire: "Greene threw out a frag." On our next strafing run I threw out the remaining grenade without waiting.

I'm not sure about the others, but I had lost track of time. And the fact was, it doesn't take long to use up your ammunition, but I knew that we were in a desperate situation and began wondering how we were going to get these guys out of there. The situation looked grim, very grim. But then suddenly, and I will never forget that deep southern drawl which came on the radio, it was the voice of the first CH-46 pilot: "Klondike, my fuel warning light just came on, and if we are going to get those folks out of there, we have to do it right now."

He and his crew had been a short distance off to the west, watching and listening to this whole ordeal. I didn't give it much thought then, too busy with all that was going on, but later on in life I think back to what the crew of that 46 must have been contemplating: Is this the day

I'm going to die? But the fact was, this was what they did just about every day in Nam, helping the Marines on the ground, pulling Marine Recon teams out of harm's way.

With the 46 pilot's announcement, I'm sure that all eyes went immediately to our fuel gauges and ammo supplies. We had very little 7.62 machine gun ammunition left, and all our rockets had been fired; I had fired the case of M-79 rounds and had thrown out the three hand grenades; and if lucky, we only had 15–20 minutes of fuel left, and we were at least 10 minutes away from Khe Sanh. The pilot came on the intercom: "Greene, see if you guys can gather up what remaining short belts of M-60 rounds and see if we can get enough to load up one gun on each side, and do it fast."

For the next few minutes, the gunner and I scrambled to gather up and link together every remnant of the 7.62 ammo belts. There wasn't very much but we were able to load up a gun on each side with perhaps 150–200 rounds. Then the pilot asked the other pilots, "Are we ready?" With the affirmative response from the other birds, the pilot radioed the 46 pilot and told him that the gunships were going to stay together this time, and stay on his left side, trying to protect him from any fire from the top of the hill. He then added, "We are very low on ammo, but we'll give you everything we got for one final strafing run. Start your approach when you are ready."

The 46 had already started flying toward us when he announced his fuel situation, and as soon as we were all together, we started for the top of the hill. I don't recall how long the external guns lasted, but I remember firing all six bullets in my .38 sidearm. The 46 had circled around from the east and flew directly in on the downhill side and set down hovering on his rear wheels just below the burning helicopter, using it as a smokescreen, while slowly gathering up the other 46 crew and Recon team on board. It seemed like forever but finally the 46 lifted and pulled away to the south and then quickly turned back to the northeast, and all five Marine helicopters made a mad dash for Khe Sanh.

I remember sitting back trying to relax; all four of us in my bird kept looking at each other, trying to smile that we had just pulled off a very unlikely feat, while trying to digest what had just happened. But there was still one big question, and all eyes fixed on the fuel gauge: Could we make it back to Khe Sanh? If we went down, we would be defenseless on the ground as this whole area was crawling with NVA. After a few more minutes, we finally came within sight of Khe Sanh, and I knew there was a collective sigh of relief. And once again, that was when that deep southern accent, the 46 pilot, came back on the radio, "Klondike, great job," and then he reported that everyone aboard the downed 46, the crew and the Recon team, all had been wounded, and that they were all still alive. Finally, just minutes later, we were landing beside the airstrip at Khe Sanh. We had made it back. Just a second or two after we landed, one of the gunships behind us (I think Corporal Evans' bird 4-3) ran out of fuel while coming to a landing hover and fell the last several feet for a hard landing. We had been so lucky, but we made it.

After we had touched down and I tied down the rotor blade, I started to walk back and check on the guys on the 46, but I remember Corporal Harris came walking toward me; he stopped and said, "You don't want to go back there." So, I didn't.

To this day I think back and think about how improbable it was to get those Marines out of that situation. But that was a good day. I will never forget the voice of that second CH-46 pilot; he sounded like an older man, but perhaps he wasn't much older than I was back then, but I'll never know. That event was early summer 1967, and I had 7–8 more months to go. It turned out to be my first real "shit sandwich," a term that all Vietnam helicopter flight crews would become very familiar with; every flight crew in the squadron would have their fair share of shit sandwiches. But one of the most frightening aspects of that mission was running out of ammo, and I vowed that day that I would always save at least one 100-round box of 7.62, just in case.

You may wonder why the lead pilot, my pilot, did not decline to attempt the second Recon insert with suspicious enemy activity at the LZ site. I know that he struggled with his dilemma, but it was not his decision to make. All ears were listening to the radio conversations, but whether or not the Recon team leader had consulted with his superiors, we'll never know—Recon teams had their own radios and their own frequencies. In my old age, and after writing about this event,

I have been pondering, "What if we hadn't make it back to Khe Sanh that day?" We had very little fuel, flying on fumes with scant minutes before all five helicopter engines started shutting down. Klondike 4-3, Corporal Evans' bird, just barely made it back. We were all so lucky. If we had not made it, what a calamity it would have been. Most likely each helicopter would have started falling out of the sky individually, and at different locations. Helicopters can land safely without engine power by auto-rotation, but not over very tall trees and heavy jungle. It would have been a catastrophe for 30–35 of us Marines. If we had survived the crash we would have found ourselves separated on the ground, with a third of us already seriously wounded from the NVA ambush, and no ammunition to fight with. When we passed the Montagnard village near Khe Sanh, we knew we had made it back, thank God.

Many years later, back in the 1990s, when I found out about the "Pop-A-Smoke" reunions and the Vietnam Helicopter Association, my wife and I were able to attend five or six reunions. On each of those occasions, I visited all the CH-46 squadrons and attempted to locate that pilot, and/or possibly a crew member of that fateful day, but have had no luck whatsoever. After 50-plus years I have oftentimes thought about what the CH-46 pilot and his crew were thinking that day, seeing their wingman getting shot down at close range by NVA fire; watching us trying to neutralize the situation; and then putting their lives on the line attempting to safely land next to the burning helicopter and get their squadron mates and the Recon team out of that hellish situation; then all five helicopters racing against time and very little fuel.

Another significant aspect of that Marine Recon mission is that if had we been dispatched out on SOG missions that day, the Marine Recon teams and the CH-46s most likely would have been escorted with just one section of gunships (two helicopters instead of four) with only half the ordnance that we had. For whatever the reason, the "King Bees" did not show up, and that turned out to be a very fortunate event. It probably would have been a different outcome had it been the typical Marine Recon mission. But that was what all Marine helicopter crews did, day after day in Vietnam, and it was one of many, many days that I was so proud to be in the USMC Aviation with them. Semper Fi!

I took a lot of photos during my time in Nam, but sadly not many of the guys in the squadron. One of the very few photos of pilots that I took was of Captain Bobby "Gabby" Galbreath. The photo was taken at Khe Sanh during another mission; Gabby had been my pilot that day, and we had just parked the bird and were spending the night at Khe Sanh. Gabby was one of the older pilots, a nice gentleman who always had a smile on his face. I believe that he was originally a warrant officer. He could have been one of the other pilots that day that we got the Recon team and 46 crew out, but there is no way of knowing for sure.

Sadly, Gabby and Crew Chief Corporal Harry Schneider, a regular on the SOG missions, and two others were killed in action up in the DMZ just a few days after I left Vietnam during the Tet "cease fire" in early

Capt. Galbreath at Khe Sanh.

February 1968. Captain Galbreath and crew—Lieutenant Paul Jensen, Gunner Staff Sergeant Jimmy E. Tolliver, and Crew Chief Harry W. Schneider—were the chase bird on an emergency Recon team extraction in the DMZ. I never found out all the details, but the squadron gunships had been making strafing runs in support of (I think) CH-34s, but the 34s were under heavy enemy fire and could not hold the whole team, leaving several Marine Recon still on the ground.

Captain Galbreath and crew decided to use up their remaining munitions to reduce weight and tried to rescue the last two or three team members. After expending their rockets and most of the 7.62 ammunition they landed and were lifting out of the LZ with the remaining Recon team, when their bird was struck by a heavy burst of NVA fire and crashed. I was told that the NVA fire might have hit the engine causing them to lose power as they were lifting out of the zone. And when they hit the ground, the bird rolled over on the left side and pinned Crew Chief Corporal Schneider under the helicopter. The Recon guys sitting in the middle of the bird landed on top of him, as they had also been wounded.

The NVA were immediately on the crash site and shot everyone still alive in the head, but they apparently did not see Schneider.

Corporal Harry Schneider (left) with Pete Harris at Phu Bai.

They think that Schneider had either passed out or played dead. At daybreak the next morning the QRT (Quick Reaction team) arrived and discovered that Harry was still alive, and finally got him out, but he died shortly thereafter.

CHAPTER 11

A Hard Day's Night

Later in the spring of '67, MACV ordered a "max effort" to provide all available aircraft to the helicopter squadrons in the I Corps area for a major operation northwest of the Tam Ky area. We were up at 0330 hours and scheduled to depart Ky Ha an hour later with my pilot that day, squadron Commanding Officer Lieutenant Colonel Joe Nelson. We were the lead gunship and at first light we were scheduled to be over the area of the operation to check the weather conditions; Lieutenant Colonel Nelson would decide if the operation was a "go" or a "no go." The area of the operation was in the foothills west of the small airstrip which was west of the town of Tam Ky. VMO-6 assigned a section of gunships to this airstrip every day on standby.

There were several squadrons with dozens of transport helicopters and many hundreds of grunts on standby waiting for Colonel Nelson's decision. We were over the landing zone area with clear skies at daybreak when he radioed Land Shark that the operation was a "go." We headed back to the airstrip to top off our fuel tanks and waited for the transport birds with troops to arrive.

I don't remember how many sections of gunships the squadron had there that day, but the sky was swarming with all the different types of Marine helicopters for most of the day. I don't recall that there was much resistance from the VC and NVA that day; I suspect that when they saw all the helicopters overhead, they must have headed for their underground tunnels, or hightailed it for Laos. But wave after wave of grunts were landing in the LZ, then spreading out, and later the CH-53 transport choppers started bringing in supplies and heavy artillery. It was a busy day, but not a lot of serious gunfire as I recall.

All day long, gunships took turns rotating around the outer perimeter of the LZ, in case of trouble, and refueling at the Tam Ky airstrip nearby. Late that afternoon it became apparent that a storm was brewing and soon would be coming down out of the mountains. Colonel Nelson decided to send the other gunships back home to Ky Ha, but we stayed, with our chase bird, until the end of the day. It was almost dark when and had started raining as we departed for Ky Ha.

We had no sooner got started when Colonel Nelson discovered that we had lost our TACAN (an instrument which helped us find our way back to Ky Ha in poor visibility), so we headed straight east for the South China Sea. When we found the coastline, the ceiling was down to about 500 feet with heavy monsoon rains. With such poor visibility, we stayed out about 50 yards out over the water and followed the surf as it was crashing down on the shoreline because the coast north of Ky Ha was mostly hills, and an occasional mountain. It was not an easy trip as we were flying over "Indian country" (VC territory) with very low cloud cover, little visibility, and about 50 feet above a very angry ocean. I'm sure that all eight of us were a little on edge with only the pounding surf to guide us back to Ky Ha.

Finally, we started to see the lights ahead and the boat harbor on the north end of Ky Ha; we had made it back to "home, sweet home." It was about 2130 hours, and it had been a very long day. Once the CO had parked the bird in a vacant space, he and the co-pilot, as well as the gunner were done; their day was over. However, the crew chief must finish up his day post-flighting the bird, putting the door guns away, and putting the canvas door covers and gun covers on to keep the rain out. It was 2200 hours or later when I got back to the hooch and crawled into my cot.

About an hour later the night duty clerk arrived, and I heard, "Greene, wake up, Greene, get up. Your tail rotor is due for a 'thousand-hour inspection', and they want you to get it over the HM&S [Maintenance Squadron] right away to be x rayed." It had been a very long day, and I really didn't feel like it, but I got up, dressed, got on a poncho, and headed for the flight line. It was still raining, and I had to get some equipment out: extension cords, lights, and staging to get up at the tail rotor. Probably about 0030 hours I got the tail rotor off and over to HM&S, and then I hustled back to my cot. But it wasn't an hour or so later when the clerk was back: "Greene, get up, your tail rotor is ready, and they want your bird ready for a 0600 test flight."

Thankfully it had stopped raining, but I was up again and off to HM&S hangar. I got the tail rotor, hurried back, and reinstalled it on the bird, then safety wired it, put everything away, and no sooner did I hit the hay for the third time when the damn duty clerk was back and it was time to get up. Up again, got dressed and headed out for the flight line.

When I got out to my bird there were two avionics guys working in the nose of the bird, replacing the TACAN that had crapped out the day before. I got the fuel sample but had to skip the nose part of the inspection for the time being because the avionics guys were still there, so I continued around the helicopter performing the pre-flight inspection. I had made my way around the bird doing the routine inspection route, rechecked the tail rotor, then got up on the roof of the bird inspecting the rotor head and its various parts. When I had finished inspecting up top, and as I was climbing down off the bird on the left side, the test pilot came up behind me and asked if I was ready to go. I hadn't noticed him at any point during my inspection. He didn't even bother to climb up and inspect the rotor head himself, which we are both required to do. He seemed to be in a bad mood, probably because he didn't like getting up that early. I indicated that I was ready, and we jumped in the bird, taxied out to the runway, and he called for permission to take off. And away we went, flying out over the South China Sea, and he performed the test flight.

After he finished the test routine, he told me to take the controls while he filled out the test flight paperwork. After he finished his writing, and as we were arriving back at Ky Ha, he put out his left hand and said, "What is this all about?" He showed me some broken safety wire that the two avionics guys had apparently left behind in the nose compartment; it was then that I remembered that I never got back to inspecting the radio compartment in the nose of the bird. There was nothing that I could say, so I said nothing; I didn't offer any excuses. When we got back, he went into the ready room hooch to report the status of my bird, and I started post-flighting the bird. A couple of minutes later my section leader Sergeant Sherrill and Sergeant Hockenberry came running out, asking, "What happened?" The only thing I could tell them was that there were the avionics guys changing the TACAN, it was getting late, so I continued with the pre-flight inspection, and didn't get back to check the nose section. Sherrill and Hockenbury went back to the flight hooch. (I didn't say anything about the two avionics guys, but it was highly unlikely that they would not have picked up after themselves after changing the TACAN, unless the test pilot was a factor.) After finishing the post-flight I went to the flight ready hooch and sat down wondering what was going to happen; I was truly down. Was I going to lose my bird, get demoted, go to the brig, or worse, go on "shit" duty?

About an hour had passed when Sergeant Sherrill came back in the hooch and told me to go get my stuff out of my bird (WB#7) and put it in WB#1, and grab a change of clothes: I was going out aboard ship for two to three days. We left about an hour later. (WB#1 would be the second of three birds that I was assigned to during my tour. In late summer or early fall of the year I was on "R&R" for five days and when I returned, I was switched over to bird WB#3.)

When I got back from TAD aboard ship the guys in the section told me that the avionics techs had confirmed everything I had said, and the night clerk had reported about the ordeal that I had had during the night. That was the last I heard about it. I don't remember who the pilot was and for many years wondered who it had been. Even when I started attending the Pop-A-Smoke reunions, I wondered who he was; but in the end I decided I didn't want to know. But that was one of only two unpleasant experiences that I ever had with a pilot/officer in the squadron.

The second event was with a new pilot, a captain who was sitting in the co-pilot's seat, and it had to do with radio intercom conversation. As background information, I don't remember how the procedure got started, but I probably picked it up as a gunner watching and/or listening to how the other crew chiefs reacted on the radio when the pilot needed to hear a "confirmation" about something he was told or said to the crew chief and/or gunner. The crew chief, or gunner, would simply double-click his mike, instead of verbally responding, "Yes Sir" or "No Sir"; it was just a more efficient method than talking and tying up the radios, especially when the air waves got busy when there was action on the ground and/or helping or supporting Marines. Bottom line, it had become standard practice.

At any rate, much later in the fall of the year, this FNG co-pilot asked or told me something on the radio, and I double-clicked to acknowledge him. (Most generally a newly arrived pilot, who was sitting in the left seat up front, or the gunner for that matter, really didn't have a lot to say.) But in this case a few seconds later he asked/told me the same thing again, and as I recall it was nothing but small talk, and I double-clicked again. But the third time, he came back at me on the intercom with a loud and irritated voice, "Greene, I didn't hear a 'Yes Sir'!" It was then that I realized that he was new, and very much full of himself, and just showing off his authority. This time I answered, "Yes Sir, and I am fully aware of the situation, SIR," and I said it just as sarcastically as I could. The whole situation was so far beyond the norm, and so unusual for one of our pilots to act in such a manner. After that last exchange, the pilot looked at the co-pilot, then turned around and looked at me, and I was pretty sure that it was a big grin on his face.

These were the only two issues that I had with the pilots. There were many times in my life when I wondered who those two pilots were; but years ago, I decided that I didn't care to know. The pilots that we had in VMO-6 were super. And they are certainly one of the reasons that I am alive today. Except for the SOG missions, each day the crew chiefs would check the flight schedules to see who the pilots and the gunner were for that day; and I don't remember anyone acting superior or above anyone else. There were many times when I was the junior rank in the crew; both pilots were officers, and frequently the "heavies" (SNCOs) would take turns as the gunner to keep up their flight status, or the gunner might have been a sergeant out of one of the other MOSs. We were all there doing our job, and I believe that we did it very well. And that is the reason I have decided to try and write this book.

As previously mentioned, one of the several advantages of being in the air wing was that we didn't have to go for days on end without being able to take a shower and get somewhat cleaned up. This is in no way disrespectful to the US Army or Marine ground pounders, the grunts. But it was a fact of life that when they left the confines of their base camp and went out on patrols for any length of time their bodies took a beating. The heat and humidity, the rice paddies, and in the jungle, the sweat, and consequently, in my opinion, the body odor was synonymous with the grunts. These poor guys were out in the boonies for weeks on end, and you could tell when a grunt was close by.

One day in July of 1967, I was out on the flight line under my bird working on something when I got a whiff, then a strong odor of a grunt; I looked around and saw a pair of legs of someone standing next to my bird. When I looked up into the sun on that hot humid day, there was Steve Saner, Corporal Saner USMC (MOS 0311); one of my buddies from Kentucky. One of my good friends that I hung around with, drank beer with and chased the girls with, before the USMC and Vietnam. What a surprise.

Steve had been the first of my three Marine friends to enter the USMC, reporting to the draft board on January 5, 1966. Back in January of '66 amid the draft situation, we had lost contact with each other. Steve graduated from boot camp and ITR, and was assigned a 0311 MOS (Infantry), he was given 30 days' leave, then ordered on to "WEST PAC"—Vietnam. On arrival in Da Nang, he was assigned to B/1/5 (1st Battalion 5th Marines) in June 1966.

Steve's 5th Marines had base camps on Hills 54 and 51, which were located northwest of the Chu Lai Air Base there, and their TAOR (Territorial Area of Responsibility) was an area which we flew over and supported numerous times. And I'm sure that there were numerous missions in that area when we probably were supporting Steve and his platoon or company when they were in trouble, but never realized how close together we were. During that time, I'm sure that there were times when Steve and the other Marines were looking up at Hueys flying by, while I was looking down, and neither realized that we might have been looking at each other, with no way to know it.

Pre-flighting, birds ready to go at Ky Ha.

Main gate, Ky Ha.

PX, Ky Ha.

North perimeter Ky Ha.

VMO-6 off on another mission.

Headed on a mission south of Ky Ha.

Behind my hooch at Ky Ha.

Low tide on reef at Ky Ha.

South Koreans "loading up" supplies at Ky Ha.

My bird.

Working on bird.

Not your ordinary Chevy 409 engine.

Ordnance guys cleaning and rearming the bird.

Corporal Schoenherr repairing battle damage.

Directing air strike.

Re-supply mission to outpost southwest of Chu Lai.

I doubt these guys needed anything to keep them awake at night.

Marble Mountain, helping out VMO-2.

Waiting for mission at Phu Bai.

Highway 9 and Qua Viet river, heading for Khe Sanh.

Khe Sanh.

More views of Khe Sanh.

SOG missions at Khe Sanh.

Montagnards helping us re-arm at Khe Sanh for a SOG mission.

Montagnard village west of Khe Sanh.

Klondike 4-1, flight of four SOG.

Special Forces camp at Phu Bai.

RVN Boot Camp located next to SF camp at Phu Bai.

With RVNs at Phu Bai.

Children from orphanage just north of Special Forces camp at Phu Bai, and school nearby.

The beginning of the famous "Hill Battles" at Khe Sanh, April–May 1967. Marine grunts heading up toward Hill 861 at Khe Sanh in early April 1967, taken from the airstrip while we were waiting for the arrival of the SOG teams.

Grunts find NVA white phosphorus on Hill 861. Unfortunately we couldn't help when they ran into an ambush because we were in the middle of a SOG mission.

Air strike on Hill 861, Khe Sanh.

CH46s landing to pick up recon teams at Da Nang.

The remote outpost, "Tiger's Tooth," two miles north of Khe Sanh, in an extremely mountainous area.

View from Huey.

The only time I managed to take photographs during live strafing and rocket fire was when we were trying to assist a downed Huey in late summer 66 (chapter 14).

Trying to even the score.

No one's putting their head out down there.

Patching shrapnel holes in the tents and building bunkers at Quang Tri.

Chow Hall at Quang Tri.

White phosphorus, used to mark a target during an air strike, beyond the west perimeter at Quang Tri.

Camp Carroll.

Some RVNs were stationed at Camp Carroll and their families were allowed to visit during the day but had to return to their villages at night.

Camp Evans.　　　　　　　　　　USO show at Camp Evans.

Arc Light, B52.

Con Thien, DMZ.

Klondike on station, Con Thien.

Working the DMZ.

Not all hard work—squadron party, summer 1967.

With my orders to go home, end of January 1968.

VMO-6 challenge coin.

Today, with my medals.

With my daughter Lt Col Pamela Unger (ret) and son-in-law Major Mark Unger (ret) on the occasion of Pam's retirement from the Marines, June 2024.

It was long after Vietnam when Steve opened up and began telling me about his time in Nam. For many years, he has been quiet about his time there. Throughout his 13-month tour with 1/5 Steve had been involved with numerous squad-, platoon- and company-sized patrols and ambushes on a regular basis to ensure the safety of Hill 54, while denying the VC access to attack the Marine Air Base at Chu Lai and the helicopters at Ky Ha. In April 1967 Operation *Union One*, the objective to find and destroy the VC and their supplies in Que Son Valley, was a major battle that lasted for 27 days, but that also cost 110 Marines killed and 473 wounded. There were 865 VC confirmed killed.

In August '66, Steve was the point man on the first day of Operation *Colorado*, a regimental-size operation. Later that day they entered a village that contained the headquarters of an NVA regiment and engaged the enemy at close range, destroying their command post but losing seven Marines and 27 wounded.

On that hot and humid summer day in July 1967, Steve was getting "short," late in his 13-month tour, and flew to Ky Ha because of a toothache, or maybe faking one. Steve and his outfit had just got back to their base camp after more than a month in the bush. Someone back home must have told him about my squadron, plus all the Marines in the area knew where the helicopters were located, with some medical services available. Steve was able to stay with us in my hooch for several days. I was not able to visit all that much because of my daily flight schedule, but the other guys in the hooch took care of him during the day while I was away. And apparently the squadron SNCOs became aware that a grunt stranger was staying in our hooch, and that we were high-school friends, and allowed it to happen; Steve was a Marine, we were buddies from Kentucky, and he was "short" and going back to the world soon.

The day before he had to leave and get back to his unit, the heavies arranged for me to have the day off, and we had the opportunity to swim and dive in the South China Sea right below my hooch. The reef below our living quarters there jetted out into the ocean for about 50 yards with all kinds of exotic fish, with white sandy beaches on each side; it was truly a beautiful place, except for the fact that there was a war going on. It would be the second time that I was able to swim there.

Kentucky friends in Ky Ha.

The first time had been back in January, when the four-foot sea snake chased me out of the water. But who would have thought that the two good friends from northern Kentucky would be able to meet up in Vietnam and have a day at that beautiful beach? To this day we are still the best of friends, and I visit with Steve and my friends in Kentucky a couple of times a year.

CHAPTER 12

Couldn't Find the Bullet Hole

Every day at Ky Ha, the squadron would disperse a section of gunships to different outlying points on standby to be close by when the grunts got in trouble, or for resupply missions. But almost always there was trouble somewhere in the area; very seldom did the flight crews sit for very long. It was a game of "cat and mouse" with the enemy and there were very few days when we were not in contact with the Viet Cong or the NVA.

Most generally after returning from missions, when we knew we were taking fire and getting hit, the flight crew would look over the bird checking for bullet holes. During strafing runs with four exterior machine guns plus the door guns all firing at once it was hard to hear anything else; but otherwise, most of the time when we took hits, we all knew it.

Frequently the squadron would send a section of guns north (TAD) for the day to assist VMO-2, at Marble Mountain in Da Nang. I'm not sure why they called VMO-2's base "Marble Mt." because VMO-2 was located on the flat sand right next to the ocean; it was called China Beach and it was an in-country R&R site. There were a couple gigantic, somewhat round rocks on the south end of their flight line next to the South China Sea. Across the harbor, there were several very high hills/mountains north and west of Da Nang, but I don't really know if one of them was called Marble Mt. or if a giant rock at shore's edge just resembled a big marble.

One of those times when I and my bird were part of a section of gunships sent up Marble Mountain TAD for the day to assist VMO-2, it was late in the day, and we had been out on a Marine Recon mission northwest of Da Nang. We were returning to VMO-2 to refuel/rearm before heading back to Ky Ha. We were flying about 1,200 feet above sea level, but only a couple hundred feet above the top of Monkey Mountain, and just as we passed over the top one shot rang out and the round hit the bird. We knew that we had been hit, but after landing on VMO-2's flight mat and shutting down the engine, we searched everywhere, but couldn't find the bullet hole. It was getting late, toward evening and the bullet hole was nowhere to be found. The bird had been refueled, rearmed, and with all the instruments and gauges appearing to be normal, plus considering the fact of the competitive rivalry between the two squadrons, the pilots decided that we would return to Ky Ha.

That following morning back at Ky Ha, while pre-flighting the bird, I crawled under the bird to get the daily fuel sample, it was then that I discovered a slight fuel leak under my side of the bird and found the bullet hole right next to the tank drain valve. It had hit about two feet behind me and penetrated through the outer skin of the helicopter and into the fuel tank. Obviously, when the bullet hit, there had been sufficient fuel left in the tank to slow the bullet down so that it didn't cause further damage. The fuel tank on the Huey is located right behind the crew chief on the left side of the bird, and in Vietnam the UH-1E's fuel tanks were made of rubber and were self-sealing when a bullet found its way into the tank. However, the tanks had to be changed whenever they had been penetrated by a bullet because the sealant contaminates the fuel. So, I wasn't flying that day, and later that afternoon when I got the old tank out, there sitting on the bottom was the .30 cal round that had been shot at us.

It doesn't happen often, but in combat and under certain situations, perhaps in a hospital when a doctor pulled a bullet out a wounded Marine or soldier and decided to give it to him, that wounded Marine would have had a souvenir that I'm sure he would keep the rest of his life. I don't believe that there are too many people during Nam who had the bullet that was shot at them; but I did, and I had a unique souvenir for my time in Nam. I took the bullet over to the HM&S squadron, drilled a hole through it, and attached it to my dog tags. When I got home from Nam, I told my two youngest brothers (eight and 10 years old) not to take that bullet off the dog tags. Well, guess what, of course they did, and then lost it… Thank you, John and Mark!

CHAPTER 13

Night Standby

As is customary in military life, everybody in the squadron was divided into different sections; the crew chiefs, as well as the rest of the MOSs. The birds numbered WB#1–7 and their assigned crew chiefs were section 1, WB#8–14 was in section 2, and so on. Each section would have to provide crews for duty on night standby every fourth night. The pilots had the same arrangement and had to provide pilots for night standby. But mostly the night standby crews would just sleep in the ready room, unless there was an emergency somewhere, or someone was in trouble and needed air cover; but generally, there were not many calls, so the night standby crews would just try and get some shuteye in the ready hooch.

One day after returning from an outlying point, when we arrived back at Ky Ha the crew that I had been with that day had already taken off, no doubt headed for the mess hall. I was doing a post-flight inspection on the bird when I was informed that it was my turn for night standby, and my next crew was waiting for me to check in with the post-flight report. The fuel truck guys had arrived and were refueling the bird. This was going to be an immediate return to duty, and we were heading back out as soon as the new crew got on the bird. No time to go to the mess hall for dinner; it was going to be more C-Rats for me.

My next pilot was again the senior officer, so we were the lead. The chase bird crew had been waiting, and as soon as my bird was given a pre-flight inspection and refueled, we took off and headed south. We were relieving the day standby, who had been flying shotgun, watching over some M60 armored tanks since earlier in the day. I don't remember if it was two or three tanks, but they were out there in the South Vietnam countryside without ground support, by themselves, and for reasons unknown to me, the lead tank had become disabled; probably it had either hit a mine, or became immobilized, but the tanks were stuck and could not move forward.

When we arrived on-site, the day standby returned to Ky Ha after they passed on the sitrep, which was essentially that the tanks were trying to cross over a causeway to get to the other side of a river. How long the tanks had been there, or what had stopped them earlier in the day, wasn't mentioned; there was no time to fill me in. Perhaps the rest of the night standby relief crews had been briefed before I joined, I don't know.

I suspected the tanks must have been heading in the direction of the Korean Marine camp, or perhaps the air facility at Chu Lai. But I remember well, and I couldn't imagine why they were traveling in the Vietnam countryside alone without ground support, or why Marine Headquarters had not dispatched a Quick Reaction Team (QRT) in to provide support. But before we knew it, we had been flying shotgun over them for almost two hours, checking the surrounding area for any enemy activity, and it was about 2000 hours, and night coming on. The fuel gauge indicator was getting low when the pilot notified the tank crews that we had to return to base to refuel, and we headed back north. He also notified Land Shark and Ky Ha and indicated that we needed a "hot" refuel, and then an immediate turnaround.

After refueling and on our way back, the tanks were still in the distance several miles away, when suddenly the tank radioman came on the airwaves screaming that they were under attack. Looking ahead we could see the mortar rounds exploding all around the tanks. I remember the pilot pulling back on the collective control (for more power) and nosing the cyclic stick ahead (more speed), but what I remember most was watching the main rotor head RPM needle on its tachometer: it was way too far in the red, and I recall saying on the intercom, "Sir, the rotor head." He did back off a little bit, but we were still about a half-mile away when he started firing the four exterior guns, and a few seconds later we were back on station, shooting up the surrounding area. Night was upon us, and it was getting dark, and we could not locate the enemy; they had gone back into hiding. But for sure, those guys on the ground in those tanks were in trouble, big trouble.

The pilot called back to Klondike base and Land Shark with the sitrep, and said they should dispatch another section of guns, ASAP. For the next several hours we took turns with another section of guns flying shotgun over the tanks, but the enemy were laying low and waiting. Unfortunately, the grave situation was further deteriorating and looking northwest we could see that there was a storm brewing and coming down out of the mountains, and it had already started raining. It was about midnight when the heavy monsoon rains began with little visibility and low cloud cover. When the ceiling was down to about 500 feet, the pilot reported the situation to Land Shark, and we were ordered to return to Ky Ha.

The next morning as usual I was awakened at 0500 for that day's flight schedule. After pre-flighting the bird and back in the ready room hooch, checking to see who the crew was for the day, I didn't ask the duty officer about the tank crews; I didn't want to know. But in Vietnam, the reality was that the enemy owned the night, and that mission had become just another day in Vietnam for VMO-6 flight crews. I certainly was hoping the higher-ups had dispatched a QRT out there to help those guys in the tanks. But the fact was, and any of the flight crew could attest to this, far too often the outcome of most of those shit sandwiches that we incurred was just out of our control, and the results of those events or episodes were unknown to me.

Several weeks later it was again my section's, and my turn for night standby, but instead of the usual, an uneventful night and trying to get some sleep in the ready room hooch, Land Shark called, and we were ordered to fly southwest of Chu Lai in the foothills and mountains to help a small outpost over near the Laotian border, which was under attack by the VC and/or NVA. I believe it must have been US Army SF embedded with the local Montagnard at their camp. It was a very dark night with high cloud cover, and the camp was rather small and circular, with a flashing strobe light denoting the center of the camp; I had no idea how many of the good guys were there, but there couldn't have been a lot of people in that small camp.

A USAF flare plane was high overhead, probably out of Thailand, lighting up the night sky. There were green and red tracer rounds all around the camp which were both incoming and outgoing machine gun fire. Shortly after we arrived, we had tracers coming up at us. Generally, at night the pilots would turn down the running lights on the sides of the bird to low, so that it was difficult for the enemy on the ground to judge the bird's elevation. Of course, when the enemy on the ground started shooting at us it gave away their positions and we were able to shoot back.

Things seemed to have settled down after we arrived, and I think that we probably broke up the attack on the camp, because we returned to Ky Ha, and I don't recall Land Shark having to call for another section of guns to replace us. Missions at night were rare and dangerous, particularly in the mountains and foothills; the terrain changes so quickly, one minute you are over rice paddies, but then suddenly, you are staring at a mountain coming at you in the front window.

Another thing that needs to be mentioned and understood is that any aircraft has a limited amount of time which it can remain airborne. A Huey gunship, like any other helicopter, can carry only so much fuel, ordnance, and munition, and when the fuel gauge says it's time to leave, that is what we had to do. Most of our missions were limited to the amount of time we had, and the fuel and ammunition situation. For most of those missions, the end results were out of our control, as was the three armored tanks event.

CHAPTER 14

Last Missions from Ky Ha

Much of our work as a squadron was working with Marine Recon teams, especially when the squadron moved to Quang Tri later in the year. But another time at Ky Ha while we were on day standby, Land Shark called with a mission to assist a Recon team in trouble in an area southwest of Chu Lai in the mountains. When we arrived overhead and contacted the Recon team, we didn't know exactly what their sitrep was, whether they had contact with the enemy or had just spotted enemy movement. The terrain was thick with heavy jungle, and we could not see either the Recon team or the enemy. The team leader on the ground did not want to give away their position by "popping smoke," so their radio man guided us in over their position and told us when we were directly overhead when we flew over. With the Recon team located, they then directed us toward the vicinity where the reported enemy had been spotted.

We were the lead bird and the pilot called Land Shark and requested a flight of fixed-wing aircraft with 500-pound bombs for an airstrike. We had been there over the team only about 10–15 minutes, but in about two minutes, we had two jets overhead waiting for us to mark the target. We were getting ready to fire a couple of "Willie Peter" (white phosphorus) rockets to mark the attack area for the jets, when Land Shark came up on the radio screaming, "Klondike cease fire, cease fire." As it turned out, the Marine Recon team had run into a US Army Ranger patrol, and it was a good thing they realized what was happening and notified someone, or it would have turned into something bad. Obviously, we were in the area where I Corps and II Corps met, and just like the South

Vietnam/Laotian border, it was very difficult to know exactly where you are, when there's nothing but mountains and jungle. It's the same for Army Rangers, Marine Recon, and helicopters.

I had flown with Lieutenant Colonel "Crazy Joe" Nelson many times, as had all the crew chiefs. I recall that on one mission, he was showing a Marine general the layout of Marine bases in and around the lower part of the southern section of the I Corps area. I don't remember if we had my bird, or a Huey slick, but we didn't have a gunner on this trip, it was just Joe and me, and we were hauling around a one- or two-star general. Apparently, the general was new in Nam and just getting acquainted with the area; it was Joe and the general up in the front, with Corporal Greene in the back seat enjoying the ride.

There were several times with Crazy Joe that I recall, while returning to Ky Ha from a mission, when he would drop down to treetop level in the area between Tam Ky and Ky Ha, and he would point out to the crew where fields of marijuana were growing. Cannabis was part of Vietnamese culture. But whatever his reasons, more than once while returning to Ky Ha Joe would scout the area checking on the progress of the marijuana crop.

Regarding marijuana, while still at Ky Ha, there were a couple of times, with a different pilot and crew, that we were sent TAD for day standby up to Phu Bai to assist VMO-3. Their base was adjacent to the Vietnamese civilian/military airport, just south of the ARVN boot camp and training center, and the SF camp. Once or twice, we happened to be up there while on standby waiting for a mission, and just out of curiosity, I walked over and noticed in their terminal it was mostly civilians and RVN soldiers arriving and waiting for flights. It was nothing more than a big wide-open hangar with only an overhead metal roof, but what really struck me was the thick cloud of marijuana smoke that was always hanging there just overhead. It seemed that everyone there was smoking pot, obviously part of their culture.

Another day with Crazy Joe, we were a section of guns returning to Ky Ha after a mission when Klondike Flight Operations called "Klondike 6" (Joe) for another mission, and requested that he come to Flight Operations. We landed and stayed on the takeoff strip for the fuel truck to refuel the birds. Joe told us to stay with the aircraft and that he would be right back, and he took off running.

Several minutes later he came running back. I was holding down one of the rotor blades as he was rushing by; he said, "We're in a hurry and we'll brief enroute." Both pilots fired up the engines and we took off to the north. As soon as we got airborne, Joe got on the radio and called Land Shark informing them that we were a section of gunships heading for coordinates in an area southwest of Da Nang. Then he said that he wanted four sections of fixed-wing (eight jets) and what he wanted for ordnance, and to meet us at those coordinates. I remember when he said four sets, the gunner and I just looked at each other wondering what was going on, and what was Joe up to now.

It took us about 20 minutes to get there, but the fixed-wing aircraft were already there circling around, waiting for us. The target was a very large village in the middle of a huge rice paddy area between Tam Ky and Da Nang. During that time, I don't remember if there had been any conversation between us and the chase bird about the nature of the mission; but it was obvious to the civilians in the village, that with numerous jet planes circling overhead and two Huey gunships arriving, it was time to "Get the hell out of Dodge." Hundreds of villagers started streaming out of the village into the rice paddies. Joe informed the fixed-wing that their bombing runs would be north to south, then he nosed over, positioning the bird, fired a couple of "Willie Peter" rockets in the center of the village and told the fixed-wing, "Cleared hot on your target." In a very short period, most of the village's hooches were flattened, destroyed; mission accomplished.

Before heading back to Ky Ha, we made a low-level pass over what was left of the village to assess if there was any further need for more bombing. As we passed over the remnants, I happened to look out the right side of the bird past the gunner and noticed one of the few hooches still standing; there was a rather tall military-age Vietnamese man naked from the waist up, peeking out the open window. The mission was over, and we headed south for Ky Ha.

The following morning after pre-flighting, and getting the bird ready for the day's assignments, there was a lot of chatter in the ready room about a large-scale battle that occurred during the night, and that the night standby crews had been involved. That morning's news was about the big battle in the same area where we had conducted the airstrikes the previous day. A South Vietnamese battalion had been sweeping through the area around that village, and they had received intelligence earlier that day that the NVA were in the area, then they ran into a large NVA unit that had infiltrated the village and the surrounding area. Our mission of destroying that village the day before was just another day in the Vietnam War; whether our destroying the village helped our ARVN allies during the previous night's fight is anybody's guess. All I knew was it was another day and my bird and I were off for another day's missions elsewhere.

Just about every night after the crew chiefs returned to Ky Ha from different locations, we would briefly get together to swap stories about the events of the day flying around in the skies of Nam and interact about what excitement we had had during the day. Almost always there would be six to eight crew chiefs who had been flying earlier, and each had their own stories to tell.

One night late in the summer of '67, Corporal Phelps (from Louisville) came in and was explaining that he had just left the ordnance armory, and that he had just swapped his .38 for a .45 cal. pistol. Then he started telling us about the mission that he had had earlier that day when he had teamed up with Captains Pless and Fairfield, plus Gunny Paulson, the gunner; their assignment that day had been medevac escort. Earlier that morning while they were out on a medevac mission with the transport chopper in the southern part of the I Corps, they suddenly heard a "Mayday, Mayday," on the radio guard channel. It was a US Army gunship, a little further south, calling for help; his wingman had been shot down and the enemy were overrunning it and killing the crew on the ground. And then Corporal Phelps told us the rest of the story and the reason that he had swapped his .38 Cal pistol for a .45. I must admit that I for one, and I believe that some of the other guys were probably thinking the same thing, that he might have been exaggerating, just a little bit, but he wasn't.

Several weeks after that night, we found out how accurate Phelps' story really was. As it turned out, after Captain Pless heard the distress call, he radioed ahead to inquire about the medevac. The Marines on the ground indicated that it was not that serious, the area was mostly secure, and that the solo transport should not have any problems by itself. With that information, Pless and crew immediately headed south toward the area of the "Mayday" distress call, and responded to the caller that they were heading their way. When they arrived there, they found the downed army gunship on the ground with enemy all around it. Pless and crew immediately rolled in "hot" with the external guns to drive away the VC who were attacking the army crew, and then Captain Pless landed next to the downed army chopper. Both Gunny Poulson and Corporal Phelps jumped out and were out on the ground trying to get the wounded soldiers out of the downed chopper and into their gunship. And just like Corporal Phelps had stated several weeks earlier, he was carrying one of the wounded soldiers over his shoulders back to his gunship when a VC came charging at him; Phelps turned and fired repeatedly but had to empty all six rounds in his .38 into the gook from just a few feet before he finally went down for good. During all this, Captain Fairfield, the co-pilot, had to unbuckle and jump in back to man both door guns to keep other VC away.

Little did anyone in the squadron realize, nor did even Captain Pless and crew know, that several months later Pless would be awarded the Congressional Medal of Honor. The flight crew, Fairfield, Poulson, and Phelps were all awarded the nation's second highest award, the Navy Cross. Their story and many, many like it, was typical of what USMC Aviation did in Vietnam daily.

Once during the summer, after we had completed that day's SOG missions at Khe Sanh, we were getting ready to return to the SF camp at Phu Bai when a Special Forces major asked if he could hitch a ride with us. The major was a heavyset Black man, but what I remember most about that day was that he was carrying a very dirty M-16 rifle; the M-16 looked as if it had been dropped in a muddy rice paddy, and he hadn't had a chance to clean it, or didn't bother. If he had been a Marine with a dirty weapon like that, he would have been in big trouble, regardless of rank.

Leaving Khe Sanh, the major was sitting between me and the gunner, and about halfway back to Phu Bai in "Indian country," suddenly we started receiving enemy automatic fire from the top of a mountain on our right as we passed by. The pilot spun the bird around, doing a 180-degree turn, and started blasting the peak with our outside guns. I'll never forget the reaction of the major when those four external M-60s started hammering away; he had on no ear protection, and when the deafening roar of those guns started, it caused him to drop his dirty rifle and quickly throw his hands up to cover his ears. I never realized just how loud the noise must have been coming from not one, but four M-60 machine guns, firing simultaneously. We flight crews were always wearing helmets with ear protection inside.

But it was the first time that I had a passenger riding with us during an active fire. (The US Army transport Hueys were elongated and only had one door gun, not four firing simultaneously.) Anyway, after returning fire at the enemy and dropping his rifle, the major must have started thinking and then realized just how dirty his rifle was, perhaps wondering if it would even fire in the event we'd been shot down. He picked it up and started looking over the rifle, then asked me to ask the pilot if he could test-fire his M-16. Of course, the pilot answered "Yes"; the only people on the ground around that area were the bad guys.

I was watching the major holding the rifle. Instead of holding the top of the gun upright, he was holding it sideways, with the top of the rifle toward the front of the bird as he pointed it out toward the open door in front of me. He had it on automatic when he clicked off the safety. He must not have been very familiar with the M-16, or how fast it fires on automatic, and probably not very experienced with it. But in the automatic position, when you pull the trigger, the M-16 will spit out at least 4–5 rounds and will "climb" in the direction of the top of the rifle before you can release the trigger. The major started leaning toward the open door, the safety off, on automatic, and he was still holding it sideways. But the end of the rifle was still about 6 inches inside the bird. I started to reach out and attempted to pull it further ahead so he wouldn't shoot up the inside of my bird, but it was too late. Before he could release his finger on the trigger, sure enough, the M-16 started "climbing" sideways (toward the co-pilot's seat), and the result was he had stitched several holes in the inside panel of my bird. (And the tin knockers had some patching to do.) Clearly the SF major must have been embarrassed, but at least he knew that his M-16 would still fire.

On another day late in the summer, we were returning to the SF camp from earlier SOG missions at Khe Sanh, and were about halfway back to Phu Bai when Land Shark called and requested that we fly over to the foothills northwest of Phu Bai and assist a Marine unit that was attempting to retrieve a downed Huey gunship that I believe belonged to VMO-3. It had been shot down and the Marines on the ground were trying to get it ready for a CH-53 to fly in over the zone, hook up the Huey and haul it back to Phu Bai, but they were receiving sporadic enemy fire from either VC and/or NVA. They couldn't get close enough to the downed gunship and asked us to help them to suppress the enemy fire. The fire was coming from about 50–100 yards in the nearby foothills to the northwest of the downed chopper.

My pilot decided that we would attack from the east, which meant the friendlies were on the ground on my side and gave me the only opportunity that I had had in Nam to use my camera during live strafing and rocket fire. I was able to take a couple of photos of the event (see photo section). After we had expended our ordnance, we continued our way to the SF camp as there were a couple gunships coming from VMO-3 to assist the CH-53 getting the Huey back to Phu Bai.

CHAPTER 15

The Move to Phu Bai

Late in the summer of 1967, the squadron was alerted that we would be moving north to our new home just south of the DMZ, a new air base being constructed west of the town of Quang Tri. There was a lot of speculation within the ranks that we were going to cross over the DMZ and head into North Vietnam, and that was one of the reasons for the move. Whether or not there was any validity to the rumor, I don't know, but there is no doubt that the Chinese would have moved across the border to defend the North, just as they did during the Korean War. But the reality of the situation was the ever-increasing numbers of North Vietnamese pouring into the northern part of the I Corps area; in the end the true objective was to get the helicopters closer to Khe Sanh and the DMZ for air support needed for the Marines on the ground.

During the squadron's movements north, I'm not sure if we were returning from SOG missions, or TAD somewhere else, but instead of flying back to Ky Ha, Land Shark informed us to head for Phu Hai, our new temporary home. The whole squadron and everything in it had already been moved and had settled in at Phu Bai when we landed on that first day there. With VMO-3 also stationed there, and now our squadron, it was a bit crowded. But just like at Ky Ha, it was business as usual: they started assigning sections of guns at other outlying points including Khe Sanh during the move north. We were there at Phu Bai only a very short period, perhaps three weeks or so as I recall.

The only event that jumps out at me during our brief stay, was the day we were returning to Phu Bai late one afternoon to discover that a

Corporal Levanduski's bird at Phu Bai. Pre-flight indicated the bird is not ready, Mike got the day off.

US navy attack jet, returning from a bombing mission over the Ho Chi Minh Trail, apparently had a 500-pound bomb hung up under his wing. He had attempted to shake the bomb loose out over the ocean, then try and have it fall over the A Shau Valley, which was a short distance northwest of Phu Bai, which the NVA basically controlled.

From what I understand the pilot tried in vain to shake it off and was unsure if the bomb was still attached to his plane. I heard that he was trying to return to either Da Nang, or out aboard his ship, but couldn't attempt to land with an unsecured bomb still on board. The guys told me that he requested a "fly-by" at the Phu Bai tower, to see if they could see if the bomb was still there. He was given permission, but unfortunately, when he flew over the Phu Bai flight line and the area where our gunships were parked, that is when the bomb finally decided to let go, and made a direct hit next to WB#15, Corporal Mike Levanduski's bird. Bird #15 was destroyed.

Another day after the move to Phu Bai, we were on standby when one of the other crew chiefs came into the flight hooch and asked me, "What's that on your bird?" I had no idea what he was talking about, so we walked out on the flight line to discover that the ordnance guys had removed the regular rocket pods from my bird and had replaced them with something different. The strange pods had green plastic tarps over them to conceal them from public view, were made of clear plastic, and were the same size as the regular pods, but those pods were filled with many small 2–3-inch diameter by 6–8-inch long silver canisters. The only thing that we could think of was the canisters contained tear gas, and we were going to drop them somewhere over the nearby A Shau Valley. Nobody seemed to know anything about those strange pods and the contents or weren't allowed to say; but an hour or so later, and before I realized it, the ordnance guys had returned and replaced them with the regular pods with the high-explosive rockets. Maybe they were just trying them on for size; anyway, there was little to no conversation about the event, it had become a dead issue.

Prior to our move further north, we had several occasions to stop at Phu Bai to refuel and rearm while on daily missions, but other than the 500-pound bomb and the mysterious pods on my bird, I don't remember much about our brief stay with VMO-3 at Phu Bai, other than it seemed to rain most of the time. However, sometime during August or September, I received a letter from my mother that she and my stepfather had divorced, that her grandfather (Papa) had passed away, and she had moved the family back to Maine to be near her relatives in Monticello. At that time there were six kids: two of my younger brothers who were still in high school, and four stepbrothers and sisters who were all under 10 years old. It was certainly unwelcome news but obviously there was nothing that I could do about it, I was only halfway through my tour. There was too much going on here in Nam to dwell on it, but still, it was bothersome and looking ahead, I was not too excited about returning home only to have to help support the rest of my family for the next decade. When we were growing up both my brother Dick and I, as the two oldest youngsters in a large family, had been put to work at a local grocery to help put food on the table, and I was not looking forward to that same situation when I rotated home after Nam. I had been looking forward to getting back home to Kentucky, where I grew up and where all my friends were, settling down and starting my own life.

I'm not sure if we were still at Phu Bai, or if it was after the move north to Quang Tri, but one day when there were sufficient gunships available for assignments, they decided to send two of the birds down to the nearby city of Hue to practice using the Huey's electric hoist. We practiced in the enclosed walls of the Citadel. During my entire tour in Nam, I had never had the need nor the opportunity to use the hoist, but it was located on the right side on top of the bird; the controls were on the ceiling in front of the gunner's seat. The pilot kept the bird in a hover of about 25–30 feet above the ground while I hoisted a 100-pound weight up and down; we practiced for about an hour, but never had the need to use it. But I'm sure that there were many occasions deep in the jungles up north in the mountains when the CH-34s had to make an emergency extraction, hauling out a Marine Recon team where there wasn't a place to land. And it was obvious with the deteriorating situation and the ever increasing numbers of NVA around Khe Sanh and in the DMZ, that the potential for us gunships to need to use the hoist was increasingly becoming a reality.

CHAPTER 16

Quang Tri Air Base

The reason we were briefly based at Phu Bai was because the Navy Seabees had not completed construction of our new home at Quang Tri. But on both moves, the temporary one to Phu Bai and then on to Quang Tri, the other flight crews and I had been away from the squadron on outlying missions for the day when the moves were made. At the end of the day, both times, the pilots were told to fly to Phu Bai or Quang Tri; somebody else in the squadron had grabbed our personal effects (spare clothes, 782 gear, rifle, and whatever else). When we arrived, these items were already on the cots at Phu Bai where there were regular hooches; it was no big deal as we were accustomed to being away from the squadron for a day or two at a time.

However, it was a different story at the Quang Tri air base for the crew chiefs and some of the enlisted: the Seabees had not yet finished building the new hooches for the enlisted flight crews. Instead, we had to spend the first several nights sleeping in tents set up on the loose white sand which was prominent in that area. But what I remember most, and really caught my eye was the canvas tents that we briefly stayed in: they were full of shrapnel holes from previous mortar attacks. However, within the week our new hooches were finished and ready for use. Those hooches were basically the same construction as the ones at Ky Ha, but instead of concrete floors, they were built about two feet above the ground.

As I recall, the airstrip at the Quang Tri facility was built right on Highway One, which ran north and south; the highway was widened on both sides so that C-130s and larger aircraft could take off and land.

The area around where the air facility was built was flat with mostly sandy soil. Unlike Ky Ha, where we were somewhat safe from attack, at Quang Tri the enemy was only a mile away. Everything about Quang Tri was different; you didn't have to fly very far to find big-time trouble. It wasn't like the southern I Corps area, where it was primarily the VC (Viet Cong) who would hit and run, disappear, and wait for the next opportunity to strike. At Quang Tri, to our west and a little further north, just south of the DMZ, the VC and North Vietnamese were everywhere, and in large numbers. It became clear that the Quang Tri air base was built to support the Marines in the DMZ, where there were four outposts, and this area became known as the "Leatherneck Square."

The top two outposts of the Leatherneck Square were less than a mile from North Vietnam in the southern half of the DMZ; I never had the occasion to land there, but as a guesstimate from the air their outer most parameters looked to be perhaps two miles apart. (Moving clockwise, the four Leatherneck Square outposts were Dong Ha, southeast, Cam Lo, southwest, Con Thien, northwest, and Gio Linh, northeast). All four of these fighting positions were nothing more than outposts, with no buildings or hooches; they were nothing more than fox holes, bunkers, with trench lines built all along the perimeters, and all of them were well within North Vietnamese artillery range. However, the Quang Tri air base was built just south of the NVA artillery range, at least while I was there. Also, the air base served as the western blocking perimeter for the provincial capital of Quang Tri. In addition, several klicks to the southwest of the air base there were two more USMC camps, Camp Evans and Camp Carroll, both located just west of Highway One. From the air base, Khe Sanh was located about 30 miles directly to the west toward Laos. Initially, early in the war, resupplies for the Marines at Khe Sanh were via Highway Nine, but truck convoys were constantly attacked by the NVA, who were there in large numbers on both sides of the road hiding in the jungle. Air became the only means of resupply for Khe Sanh, and Con Thien and Gio Linh.

The airfield at Quang Tri was on flat ground with the Thach Han River coming out of the foothills and mountains to the west, flowing around the southern end of the runway and then turning north on the eastern side of the base. It then flowed east toward the provincial capital, the town of Quang Tri. During my time at Quang Tri, all the living quarters, the mess hall, and other facilities were on the east side of the airstrip with the river flowing on the south and east side of the base. It had a large mess hall, about the same size as the one at Ky Ha, big enough to feed all the different helicopter squadrons, including the small fixed-wing planes that were used for aerial surveillance in the northern I Corps area. I don't remember eating very often at Quang Tri, mostly in the evenings when returning from Khe Sanh or elsewhere.

On the west side of the base and airstrip was wide-open land looking west and you could see many miles to the foothills and mountains toward Khe Sanh. A couple of klicks to the north was the Cua Viet River and then to the north and northwest was Leatherneck Square in the DMZ. I am not a military authority regarding security, but the air base was very vulnerable with only the river on the southern end and on the east side, and the wide-open spaces to the west. But it would have been difficult for large groups of VC or NVA to get to the helicopters and the small spotter planes that were stationed there. However, when the sun went down, it was lights out. And accordingly, the "around the clock" maintenance on the choppers that we enjoyed at Ky Ha wasn't going to work at Quang Tri, at least while I was there.

Camp Evans and Camp Carroll were two defensive USMC outposts located west of Highway One between Phu Bai and Quang Tri; I assume that they were there to try and keep the enemy from the Vietnamese population along the coast. We were on standby duty several times at one of the camps that had South Vietnamese soldiers also stationed there. I believe that their families were allowed to visit the camp during the day but had to leave later in the afternoon, while their South Vietnamese husbands spent the night, probably on guard duty on the perimeter with the grunts. I remember seeing their wives and children pass through security posts and head back to their villages while the soldiers stayed.

Most of our meals were C-Rations. However, on several occasions, Land Shark would let us stop at Camp Evans or Camp Carroll briefly for a hot lunch if we happened to be in their area. There were two occasions when we were returning to Quang Tri later in the day, when

Land Shark called and asked if we wanted to stop at one of the camps to catch some of a USO show that happened to be in progress. Of course, we did. We didn't get to see any big-name stars or entertainers as both locations were in very hostile territory, but it was the only opportunity that I, or probably most of us, got to see live entertainment while in Nam during our 13-month tours; one of the events was American singers/entertainers, and the other was Korean.

The one thing that we all realized for certain was that the relative safety of Ky Ha was no longer. While at Ky Ha, I recall only a couple times that the VC was able to lob a mortar round or two in on us. I am only guessing but I believe that they were trying to hit the helicopters which were parked close together at Ky Ha. One direct hit on the choppers would have caused a lot of damage because the area was small with three squadrons bunched together. The mortar rounds they managed to hit us with caused little damage and the only casualty that I can remember was the gunnery sergeant with shrapnel in his butt. But the air base at Quang Tri was entirely different, it was in "Indian" country, located on flat ground for miles around with lots and lots of VC and NVA all around us, waiting for the opportunity to throw mortars or rockets at us.

Early one morning in the fall of 1967, my bird and I were on day standby at Quang Tri, when Land Shark called and had ordered us to fly southwest toward Phu Bai for a mission. The previous night we knew that there had been a big fight at either Camp Evans or Carroll, because the sounds of explosions and bombings had made us aware. I don't know if the night standby had been dispatched or not.

As mentioned earlier the squadron had a good deal of missions working with Marine Recon; this was true while at Ky Ha and especially so working out of Quang Tri in the area to the west and around Khe Sanh. And I must reiterate a statement of fact, that Marine Recon did not get the recognition that they deserved during the Vietnam War. I have the utmost respect and admiration for the role they played; just imagine, small teams, of perhaps six to eight Marines, being dropped into mountains and jungle to locate, spy on, and report enemy forces and their activities up and down the western side of the I Corps area. I'm sure that the VC, and especially the NVA, had posted lookouts on the higher elevations overlooking potential drop zones and then reported those locations when and where we were inserting the Recon teams. Once on the ground it then became the deadly game of hide and seek; but eventually the Recon teams were discovered, or ran out of their supplies, and had to call for extraction. Most of the time, in the later portion of my tour, they were mostly emergency extractions with the team in contact with the enemy.

In the upper portion of the I Corps area, anywhere around the Khe Sanh area, along the Ho Chi Minh Trail, or in the highlands in the western portion of the DMZ, it became routine to insert Recon teams on the ground, then within an hour or so, we had to go back and get them out because of the large numbers of NVA throughout the entire region. There were numerous times when we were sent to help/support a team in trouble when we could not even see them because of the heavy foliage and thick jungle. We would be flying around looking for them and they would listen for the sound of our helicopters, and then direct us to them; when we happened to fly over, they would indicate that we were directly overhead. There were a couple of times while looking for a team on the ground, or trying to determine wind direction, when we had to tell them to pop a green or yellow smoke grenade, then suddenly two green or yellow smoke grenades would appear in different places, and we would have to try to determine which ones were the Marines, and which were the bad guys.

CHAPTER 17

Young Vietnamese Girl

One of the missions that I think about often is a day when my bird and I were the lead on day standby at Quang Tri in early fall of '67. That day happened to be National Election Day, and the South Vietnamese government had issued a nationwide curfew, meaning that nobody was to venture outside of their villages, towns, or cities; the only exception to the curfew was permission for its citizens to leave their homes to go out and vote.

About midmorning on election day, Land Shark called to have a section of guns fly over to the southwest of Quang Tri to investigate possible enemy activity, and indicated that artillery had already been called in. We were on standby that day, so we saddled up and flew perhaps 5–6 klicks toward the mountains west of Camp Evans. It was there that we found a small village in the foothills which had a narrow footpath leading west up to the edge of the taller mountains. Not far from the village, we also found about six to eight bodies on the path; obviously the results of the artillery that had been called. But also, along the path there were about a dozen stacks of wood; those poor villagers had only been out in the nearby woods gathering up firewood.

After a couple of passes looking around the area, we spotted one of the victims was still alive and moving. We dropped down to treetop level for a better look and it looked like a young kid. We knew that there was a high probability that at least some of the villagers were Viet Cong, and still around in the area, but it was just a young kid, and still alive, and needing medical attention. The pilot told our chase bird to cover us, that we were going to try and land, and pick up a wounded kid. However, it was not going to be easy; because of the narrowness of the path leading back to the village, and the surrounding foliage, there was very little room to land. But the pilot carefully managed to touch down with the ends of our rotor blades clipping the tops of the surrounding vegetation. He told the gunner to get out and go around the front of the bird, and grab the victim, and ordered me to shoot anything that moved. When we got the kid aboard, we discovered that it was a young girl, maybe 10–12 years old, not much younger than my youngest granddaughter today. She had shrapnel wounds on her chest and face, and a portion of her skull was exposed. The pilot lifted the bird straight up and we headed straight for the civilian hospital in the town of Quang Tri. On the way, the pilot radioed to the chase bird to head back to the air base, and that we would be right along. He called the RVN hospital and told them we had a seriously wounded young girl aboard, and we were five minutes out.

It was about noon time when we landed on the hospital helipad. The gunner and I placed the little girl on the ground, and then we waited. And we waited. The temperature, as was normal, was 100-plus degrees with the hot sun beating down on her. After a few minutes and no sign of the medical staff coming out, the pilot got back on the radio and screamed at them to get someone out there and help this little girl. A few minutes later two very effeminate-looking Vietnamese men dressed in white came out smoking cigarettes, as if out on a leisurely stroll; they finally came upon the girl, both looking down at her without a bit of urgency, never bothered to even check her, and then casually walked away.

The pilot looked at the co-pilot, then back toward the gunner and me, with anger in his eyes and a disgusted look on his face, then yanked back on the collective and we took off for the base. Nobody said a word. All I remember about that day was that little girl dying under the hot sun, with the South Vietnamese flag drooping down on the flagpole in the background. She and those villagers died gathering some firewood.

CHAPTER 18

Technical Problems

On one memorable mission, we were on standby when Land Shark reported a Marine Recon team was in trouble and needed an immediate extraction southeast of Khe Sanh. We took off with my bird as the lead. We found the team's general location but couldn't see them. On this occasion, they had no choice but to "pop a smoke" (smoke grenade), because the VC/NVA were dangerously close, and about ready to overrun them. We could tell by tone of the radio man's voice that his team was in trouble, and as soon as we were close he said that they were popping a green smoke grenade to indicate their location. And then they threw a red smoke grenade in the direction of the enemy, and said we needed to immediately start firing rockets just 50 meters east of the green smoke and their location. The pilot fired a couple of high explosive rockets about 50 meters to the east of the green smoke, and immediately the radio man came back on the air very excitedly: "Keep them coming... Klondike keep them coming... they're right on target." After we pulled out of our rocket run, the chase bird also fired two more rockets in the same area. We were rotating back around to follow the chase bird when he had completed his rocket run, and the Recon radio man came back on the air again very excitedly: "Klondike, keep them coming, you're right on target." Both birds completed another rocket run, with the same results, and the team radio man repeatedly saying the same, "You're right on target."

Then after our chase bird pulled away from his second run, we started our third pass over the attack area. The pilot fired two more rockets;

but this time the rocket on my side malfunctioned when it came out of the tube (one of the four guiding fins on the rear of the rocket, that keep the rocket going on a straight path, either broke off or failed to deploy) and suddenly we watched in horror as it veered off course to the left, and right into the area of the Recon team. Immediately the radio man on the ground started screaming, "Cease fire, cease fire." It was obvious what had happened.

Unfortunately, I don't know what transpired after that, other than the pilot notified Land Shark of the sitrep; the team was in trouble, we had no visual on them, the pilot reported that he was certain that there were WIAs, but our fuel situation indicated that we could stay no longer. I don't recall exactly where this mission occurred, but it seems to me that it was between Phu Bai and Khe Sanh. I'm sure that Land Shark had been monitoring the entire radio conversation between us and Recon team, and probably had already called for another section of guns, if one was available, and transports for an emergency extraction for the team.

However, there was nothing more that we could have done for them. It was unfortunate, but every now and then a rocket coming out of the tube would malfunction and stray off-course, hitting where it was not intended. Those events were rare occasions, and mostly it did not matter as the errant rocket would hit wide of the target; but unfortunately, this time, it did matter. And there was nothing that we could do about it. As any of the guys in the squadron can attest, it was not a very comforting feeling that we had to leave the battlefield knowing that there was nothing more we could do to help our fellow Marines, who were caught in a desperate situation; we could only hope our replacement section and the transport choppers had come to their rescue and got them out of there.

For the most part, when at Khe Sanh, we had to perform the duties of rearming and reloading the rockets into the pod ourselves, whether on the SOG or the Marine Recon missions. And most of the time, we were always in a hurry to get back in the sky as the Recon or the SOG team were in trouble. I mention this because pulling off that heavy gauge wire could easily disable or damage one of the guidance fins. And there is a high probability that is what happened during the above Recon team mishap.

On most occasions the limitations of the helicopter came into play and the UH-1E gunship was no different; we could carry only so much fuel and/or ammunition. When the squadron was stationed at Ky Ha, the southern end of I Corps, refueling and rearming was much more expeditious when we could stop at Ky Ha, Tam Ky, or Da Nang and be back in the sky and on station in a minimal amount of time. But the move north changed all that; refueling/rearming was at Quang Tri, Khe Sanh, or as a last resort, Dong Ha. Operating anywhere around Khe Sanh meant you had to return to Khe Sanh to re-arm/refuel, and at Khe Sanh there was only one section of gunships, and that was us, and there was no time for relaxing or taking your time, not when friendlies were in trouble, and we needed to get back in the fight. And, as always, both Khe Sanh and Dong Ha were within North Vietnamese artillery range, and the sight of helicopters landing at either location invited the NVA's artillery fire.

Later in the fall, up at Quang Tri, we were out on a mission and in a firefight, everybody tending to his part of being on a helicopter gunship, when suddenly we heard a loud boom. I looked down and there was a just fired and very much live M-79 grenade spinning around on the floor in front of me. Both pilots turned around looking to see what the hell had happened, with me sitting there staring with disbelief at the gunner. An instant later, I kicked the spinning 40mm grenade out the door, then turned back to the gunner again, with my arms out, palms up, as if to say, "What the hell are you doing?" Obviously, an accident, and not sure if he was new, and/or just got too excited. Thankfully the grenade did not explode; however, the impact of the discharged 40mm grenade did make an oval circular quarter-inch-deep divot in the metal floor. As I mentioned, we were amidst an active firefight and we were all busy doing our thing; to my knowledge, there was nothing more said about the incident, or to the embarrassed and guilty gunner. It was Vietnam and "shit happens."

When we returned to Quang Tri, I immediately checked in with the Ordnance Department to find out why that grenade did not explode. According to the ordnance guys, after an M-79 40mm grenade has been fired it has to rotate 17 times before it is activated. After being activated and when it hits something it will explode. I don't know if spinning around on the floor in front of me is the same as rotating out of the M-79 barrel, but it was another close call, and I am sitting here writing this story.

Another day, on another mission up in the Quang Tri area, a Marine patrol ran into trouble with a larger body of NVA, and they called for air support. Land Shark headed us over to help the grunts in the foothills west of Camp Evans or Camp Carroll. On that day the gunner was a squadron avionics sergeant. I had never seen him before, and didn't know if he was new, or perhaps the first time out on a mission. At any rate, we were in a firefight with the enemy shooting back from different directions, and that meant the gunner was responsible for suppressing enemy fire on his side of the bird. That was especially so when a helicopter gunship had finished a rocket and/or machine gun run. (When a gunship is setting up for a rocket and/or strafing attack, depending on the surrounding terrain, the pilot at the high point of elevation of the attack noses over and dives toward the target at roughly a 30-degree angle, then pulls out of the attack much lower to the ground, and at that point the gunship is "low and slow" and is most vulnerable. Whichever direction he pulls out, either right or left, the gunner and/or the crew chief must protect the vulnerable side. Every pilot was a little different with regards to the elevation and angle of attack, much depended on the terrain and the situation.)

Using our external guns, and nosing over on our first strafing pass, I wasn't paying any attention to the gunner, as I had my own side to worry about and to protect; but as we were pulling out of the first strafing run, turning to the left, trying to climb back up in the sky exposing the gunner's side to NVA fire. I looked over and could see the gunner was not shooting, but busy trying to reload another 100-round belt into his M-60. Apparently, he had been shooting straight ahead, along with the pilot and the external guns. Realizing that there was no suppressing fire coming from the gunner's side, the pilot yelled on the intercom, "Greene, get him squared away."

Fortunately, we were gaining altitude and not taking any hits. I went over and was trying to yell in the gunner's ear (a sergeant and senior in rank),

"Do not shoot your door gun straight ahead while we were strafing straight ahead, when we pull out, you have to be ready to suppress any ground fire on your side."

Obviously when the bullets start flying, both coming at us and you firing back, plus the radio conversation with the ground unit, and/or between numerous helicopters, there can be a lot of confusion. And apparently, with all the noise and radio chatter he didn't hear a damn thing I said. We had rotated back around, ready to cover the chase bird's pullout after his strafing run, and to begin our second strafing run. The pilot again nosed over and started firing, and I looked over at the gunner, and there he was again, doing the same thing, had his head sticking out and shooting straight ahead. I grabbed a smoke grenade from the floor in front of us and threw it at the gunner to get his attention; but to no avail, it was too late. We were again pulling out of the second gun run and turning low and slow, and there was the gunner again, frantically trying to reload his M-60, and all we could do was to listen as several NVA rounds were hitting the tail boom.

Fortunately, neither the engine nor the transmission, nor any of us were hit. When we got back to Quang Tri, the tin knockers easily patched over the bullet holes, which caused no serious damage, and the bird was ready to go. But it would be the only time I can remember that we had someone who was unqualified sitting over there on the right side; he was an E-5, and clearly new to what he was supposed to be doing as a gunner on a UH-1E Huey gunship. Maybe it was his first time out; hopefully he learned.

Another scary event occurred when we had been working in the western DMZ area (probably a Recon insert) and did not have sufficient fuel to make it back to Quang Tri, so we were forced to stop at Dong Ha. Under those circumstances, the pilot would not shut down the engine, only the crew chief deplaned to refuel the bird in case we suddenly had artillery rounds falling around us, and we had to immediately get airborne. (Also, as a word of note: officially, it is/was against naval regulations to refuel aircraft, and in this case a helicopter, with the engine running; but this was a time of war, and obviously the author who wrote that regulation had never flown in the Vietnam DMZ, and almost out of fuel.

But at any rate, we did what we had to do.) However, little did we know that because of the artillery threat, Dong Ha had decided to jack up the pressure on the fuel lines so that it was quicker to refuel helicopters landing there.

As soon as we landed, I jumped out and grabbed the fuel hose, opened the cap of the fuel tank (which is located right behind the crew chief's side of the bird), stuck the fuel nozzle inside the tank, and squeezed. Before I knew it, the pressure of the JP-4 coming out of the nozzle pushed me backward with the nozzle still in my hand, and before I could release the nozzle trigger, the whole rear left side of the bird was covered with fuel; and all I saw was the steam of the cooler JP-4 coming off the cowling over the hot engine and the hot tail boom of the bird. It was a wonder I didn't catch the bird afire and explode it. The pilot was so pissed, all of us could have been killed in an explosion, but there was no way that we could have known. So, the pilot told the gunner to get out and help, and while both of us held the nozzle inside the tank we got enough fuel to get back to Quang Tri. Afterward I found out that the fuel nozzle at Dong Ha was made for a larger helicopter with a nozzle which had a threaded female locking ring that screwed onto the male counterpart of a CH-46 fuel tank; it was designed for high-pressure refueling. But not for a Huey.

Many years later, at a squadron reunion, I discovered the same thing had happened to crew chiefs and corporals Rick Ault and Art Friend, also at Dong Ha. However, they told me that in both of their situations, their birds did catch on fire—luckily there were fire extinguishers nearby. Rick mentioned that in his case, the navy tried to hang him, but not the pilots, for disobeying naval regulations. But in the end cooler heads prevailed and he didn't have to face the firing squad. It's easy for a desk jockey to visualize the correct procedure for refueling a helicopter under normal circumstances.

On another occasion, one bright and early morning there were three of us gunships getting ready to taxi out to the runway; we were heading to Khe Sanh and standby up there for the day. We were one of the chase birds, sitting in the revetment area right behind and waiting for the lead gunship to start out and lead the way. After the lead pilot received permission from the tower for us to taxi out for the runway, as we were watching, the lead bird had lifted in a 2-foot hover, when suddenly, what I saw was his tail rotor come off. Immediately the pilot lost control and went down with the Huey hitting the tarmac hard, its rotor blades and other parts breaking off and flying in all directions: the helicopter was a total loss. The navy investigators were there in no time and took eyewitness statements as to what each of us had seen. I reported what I saw: the tail rotor came off, then the bird crashed. I'm not sure what other eyewitnesses saw, or told them, but the higher-ups determined that the mast (the main shaft which runs up from the transmission up to the rotor head) must have been the problem. And with that conclusion they decided to send the 2–3 remaining available birds in the squadron down to Phu Bai, to have the masts x-rayed for possible metal fatigue.

Later that day, we flew the remaining available birds (three as I recall) down to Phu Bai to the HM&S. They had a small crane there used to lift off the rotor heads off the birds and set them down on rotor head stands, and then we pulled the masts and took them over HM&S to be tested. And once again, luck had been with me, and for whoever the future crew might be. While my rotor head was sitting on the stand, which was about 4 feet off the ground with the two blades drooping down, we had a chance to give the top of our rotor blades a good looking over. And on one of my blades, I discovered a ⅛-inch-wide crack across the entire width on the top side of one of the blades, about 6–7 feet from where it is attached to the rotor head. Normally, there was no way during routine inspections to see the top surface of the entire length and width of the blade from the ground, or to inspect the rotor head while it was sitting atop the bird. The reason for the crack was that earlier we had taken a bullet through the blade where the crack was located. It was common for helicopters to get hit in the main rotor blades, and as was the repair remedy previously, the tin knockers would just repair bullet holes in a blade by filling the hole with a filler material.

Again, with the challenging stresses and the acrobatic sessions that all Huey gunships were subjected to in Vietnam, it was only a matter of time, depending on the location of the bullet hole, until a portion of the blade broke off and gravity took over. Had the hole been closer to the outer end of the blade, it might not have been a disaster, but I'm very certain that if most of the blade had broken off, we would have been goners. At any rate, after our discovery, every time a rotor blade was hit, they decided that we had to change the blade.

CHAPTER 19

The Sniffer

By early December '67, with two months of my tour in Vietnam to go, it was apparent that times had changed. The whole situation of the war had altered, and it was very apparent that the North Vietnamese were thoroughly entrenched in the northern I Corps area. Any area west of the Quang Tri air base was a free-fire zone; see anything, shoot it. Khe Sanh was getting hit daily, as well as the four Marine outposts in Leatherneck Square in the DMZ, and Camp Carroll and Camp Evans were getting hit almost daily; though I believe that the government did not want to acknowledge it, it was obvious to us that the war was escalating.

During that time, the US navy had developed a new instrument that we called the "sniffer." The sniffer was a device with a long tube mounted on the underside of the helicopter that when flown low over the ground could pick up and measure human activity; it could detect the scent or smells that humans give off, such as urine, ammonia and other odors that I know nothing about. One afternoon the avionics people had wired it up on my bird at Quang Tri. Later that afternoon Marine Command decided that we would fly around at about 25–30 feet off the ground in the area just west of the Quang Tri perimeter and a couple miles further west; we were the lead, and we had two more gunships following overhead and behind, ready to shoot had we taken fire. Both the gunner and I were up on the door guns, safeties off, ready to shoot. We were in no man's land; see anything, shoot it! As we were flying around just above the ground, I happened to glance over at the sniffer device and noticed that the needle was literally jumping around like crazy on the display gauge, so I asked the navy technician, who was sitting between me and the gunner operating/recording it, what it meant. He answered, "*Beaucoup* gooks!" (Many VC and/or NVA.)

A day or so after the sniffer mission, the avionics guys had mounted a very large spotlight, about three feet in diameter, on the underside of my bird. Military intelligence had long suspected and then discovered the VC and NVA were using sampan-like boats to ferry war materials down the river that flowed around just south of the air base and then north and east toward the town of Quang Tri. For two nights in a row, we flew low over the river, again with two gunships following behind and overhead in case we took fire. But on neither night did we see any activity nor take any fire.

The second night the gunner and I decided to have some fun; we took two 100-round boxes of 7.62 ammo. For those of you reading this, and unaware of the mechanics of a M-60 machine gun, the tracer round is simply a bullet which has a burning compound attached, usually magnesium for brightness, so that you can see where the bullets were going. Ammo belts for AA guns and fixed-wing aircraft usually had a tracer after every four rounds. However, instead of a normal tracer at every fifth round, we each loaded our door guns with one of the 100-round belts with mostly tracer rounds. I offer no excuse for being stupid that night, other than the fact that "boys will be boys"; stupidity knows no bounds. Oh well. But it was definitely pretty cool when we opened fire with the door guns, it looked as if we had a garden hose squirting out red water. Fortunately, while we were screwing around, we did not take any enemy fire, and it was a good thing because we would have been in trouble. Shooting with mostly tracer rounds in the door guns was too hot, because at about two thirds of the belt my gun jammed, and we almost ruined one of the machine-gun barrels. Didn't do that anymore.

CHAPTER 20

Mortar Attack

Several months after we moved north we were attacked and got hit hard with mortars at the Quang Tri air base; the enemy were "firing for effect" with the first two mortar rounds. Unlike Ky Ha, Quang Tri air base was on flat-level land, perhaps 6-7 miles from the South China Sea; you could look west for many miles before the terrain started to rise into the foothills and mountains. The air base was in the middle, and the terrain beyond it was enemy controlled, especially at night. You couldn't see them, but they were there and mostly living underground. At night, they owned the general area.

There were several other squadrons at Quang Tri, and all the hooches were in rows on the east side of the runway. My hooch was right next to the south end of the runway. The other side of the runway was devoid of any buildings or structures, except for the out-house facilities; it was in an open area for a couple hundred yards from the western perimeter of the air base. Because of the threat of mortar and rocket attacks, again the rule was "lights out" after dark. The bathroom we used was located on the other side and at the end of the runway, maybe 60–70 yards from my hooch, So when you had a call of nature at night, you would take your weapon and a flashlight with you, just in case.

It was the night of December 15, 1967, I had my regular call of nature at about 2130 hours. After I finished nature's duties, and as I was coming out the door to start my walk back across the end of the runway, I heard a flare go up over on the west side of the perimeter near the river and saw it light up the night sky in the area. It was the Marines on guard duty at the wire on the southwest part of the base perimeter, and I thought that they must have spotted something. A minute or so later, when I got back to the hooch, I stopped short of the stairway for a second when another flare went up. There were only three of us in our section at that time, and once inside, I remember saying to the other guys, two FNGs, as I was ready to crash for the night, "I think that we are going to get hit tonight," and mentioned that the perimeter guards had just shot up two flares. Just seconds after I lay down, the first mortar round hit the ground on the north end of our hooch and most of its shrapnel splashed toward the northeast, then almost immediately, the second mortar round of many more hit right outside of our hooch on the south end, just a few feet from where I had just been standing watching the two flares, and the shrapnel splashed toward section 2's hooch.

In a flash, in between those first two rounds, the three of us in the hooch were hauling ass, getting out and into the bunker. I think that we must have looked like a spider, nothing but legs scrambling out the door, around the corner of the hooch and into the bunker that was situated between our hooch and section 2's hooch. After we settled down in the bunker, we wondered among ourselves how the rest of the squadron had managed with all the mortar rounds falling nearby. I couldn't be sure, but I had to believe that the enemy must be using a multitude of mortar tubes, probably two from the west, and the same, or more, from the east side of the river. There was no way to tell for sure but there had to be many locations as there were just too many explosions for too long.

Once they started, they just walked the mortar rounds right down the sandy dirt road between the rows of hooches in our living area. (Our hooch was very fortunate, because had those mortar tubes been adjusted ever so slightly to the north, instead of those rounds hitting the ground just north and south of our hooch, they would have come down right on top of the next hooch to our north and then right on top of us, and we probably wouldn't have gotten out. The next rounds would have fallen on every hooch down the rows.) The bottom line was that the gooks were "firing for effect" with the very first rounds from the area where the flares went up, and there were just too many explosions, too close together, a further distance away from us. "Firing for effect," meaning there was no need to adjust their mortar tubes, the very first rounds were on target. And obviously, the NVA/VC had already had their coordinates fine-tuned from their earlier mortar attacks.

The guys in section 2 were trying to make it into their side of the bunker, but three of them ran right into the second round as it was exploding. The bunker between the hooches was built with a double-layer wall of sandbags that separated our side and section 2's side, to minimize casualties in case of a direct hit. In the divided bunker on our side, we could hear some commotion on the other side. But we had no way of knowing about how the guys over on the other side had made out. All three of us in my hooch made it safely into our side of the bunker, but after 10 minutes or so, when the attack was over and we came out from the bunker, we found that several of the guys in section 2 didn't get to their side of the bunker; three of the guys had been hit, and badly maimed.

When the attack was over, we came out of our side and fortunately there was no follow-up ground attack, because none of us had weapons on us. I walked around toward section 2's hooch and found Corporal Armstrong lying face down in the doorway; he only made it that far. He had a quarter-inch slit and a single drop of blood over his heart, but he was dead. Corporals Evans and Levanduski were on the ground in front of their hooch with chest and facial wounds, both badly wounded. The other guys in their hooch and the next one were trying to help them. They were trying to get both of them to lay back on the ground, but both Evans and Levanduski were struggling and trying to sit upright, because neither one could breathe lying on their backs with the blood filling up their lungs.

In the darkness, I could see and hear more chaos further down the road between the two rows of hooches. But after coming out of our bunker, I was only there about a minute or so when the heavies came running, saw me and yelled, "Greene, get to your bird and get airborne." With that I suddenly came out of my daze, ran back in the hooch, grabbed my flight suit and boots, and took off running barefoot to my bird. When I got there, I started removing the gun covers and door covers, inserted the barrels in the exterior guns, and activated the rocket pods. There was no time for a pre-flight inspection, nor the normal safety procedures. Then two pilots came running up, with someone else for a gunner. We all jumped aboard; there was no time for calling the tower, or taxiing to the runway; the pilot just pulled back on the collective for power, and we lifted straight up in the night sky. We really didn't know for sure if the mortar attack was over, or if some of the enemy had penetrated the perimeter and were inside the air base, so we just got airborne. We just flew around the perimeter the rest of the night, landing only to refuel when necessary.

In the night darkness, and with the lights-out mandate, we couldn't really see much of anything within the air base's perimeter, just total dark both within the perimeter and in the surrounding area. It didn't appear that the enemy were after the aircraft; apparently their goal was concentrating their mortars on our living quarters and causing havoc among the Marines. At dawn when we landed, I checked out and inspected the bird as if it was just the beginning of a normal day. When I reported to ready hooch and signed off the bird, there were two new flight crews already waiting, one for me and the other crew for the second bird; then we saddled up and were off to the war at Khe Sanh for the day. Nobody knew much about the details of the previous night.

When we returned from Khe Sanh later that afternoon, I did the post-inspection and headed for the ready hooch, but still nobody seemed to know what the extent of the damage was, or how many WIAs there were; nobody seemed to know anything regarding the severity of the attack. I only knew for sure that Corporal Armstrong was killed, and that Evans and Mike Levanduski were seriously wounded, and nothing more. I did not know until over 30 years later, at one of the "Pop-A-Smoke" reunions, that there had been between 50 and 60 more Marines wounded that night at Quang Tri; most of those included in that number were those wounded in the other transport squadrons. It was not a good night for the USMC.

Some years later, thinking back to that night, there were only four of us in section 1 that day, which included the two FNGs in our hooch. But I remember Sergeant Nickerson, who was a short-timer in our section; he was the fourth. He wasn't very tall, but he was fiery for his size, and he reminded me of a "banty rooster." Anyway, for several weeks prior to the attack, his prized possession in Nam was a silk suit that had been hanging up next to his cot. He had bought it on R&R, and if anyone touched it, or even came close to it, there was hell to pay. Lucky for him, his 13-month tour was up, and he was scheduled to rotate home the very day of the attack. I was told that earlier in the day he had gotten ahold of some booze and was hammered most of that afternoon, and he was stumbling around in the hooch waiting for his ride on that transport helicopter to Da Nang, just 5–6 hours prior the attack. I hadn't yet returned from Khe Sanh the day of the attack, but the FNGs told me that his precious suit, that he cared so much about, was wrapped around his neck when he finally stumbled aboard his chopper ride back to Da Nang, and then back to the world. But it was his good fortune that he left when he did, as I doubt he would have made it out the door.

I remember getting back from Khe Sanh late the day after the mortar attack. There was still little information about casualties, or what extent of damage had occurred the night before, but what I did notice was all the new additional sandbags that were stacked up around all the hooches. Practically every hooch, except section 1's and my hooch. The guys in each hooch were responsible for taking care of their own and obviously, just about everyone had been busy filling sandbags and adding them on the outside of their hooch. Most all the hooches had additional sandbags stacked up 2–3 feet around the outsides of the hooch before the mortar attack; but afterward they were several rows higher. I had concluded that the two FNGs were probably out on the flight line trying to help the other crews get birds back in service, and just didn't have time to get sand hauled in and fill bags to add to our hooch. But there was nothing I could do about it.

Up early every day then off to Khe Sanh, or wherever, there was no way that I/we could fill and add more sandbags to the outside of our hooch. But I spent a lot of time thinking about a possible solution, and after a while, I came up with a good idea, not only for myself but for the other guys in the hooch. My bunk in our hooch was in the middle on the east side, and it was adjacent to the entrance of the bunker next to our hooch. After a couple of days, I decided to make an "escape door" on the right side of my bunk facing the bunker entrance. Up at Khe Sanh, the rockets that we used were transported to Vietnam in wooden crates, and there were two crude hinges on each crate. I grabbed a couple hinges off a discarded wooden box, and after getting back later that day, I borrowed a hand saw from a Navy Seabee. I cut a two-foot door in the plywood in the wall next to my bunk and made a trap door. The next time we got hit, all I had to do was to roll out of the bunk, swing open the trap door, jump down 2 feet to the ground and into the bunker. The other guys could follow behind me.

Fortunately, we did not get hit again as bad as the mid-December attack during the rest of my tour. However, there were several times in the month and a half that I had left when we thought we were under attack again in the middle of the night, with everyone scramming to get to their bunker, but most of them were false alarms that turned out to be "Arc Light" (the B-52 airstrikes), which were dropping their bomb loads just a few miles away. At any rate, they certainly felt like we were under attack, the same as mid-December, or that we were having an earthquake. The B-52 strikes were very loud and the ground shook like crazy for miles round, and my "escape door" worked perfectly.

After the squadron's move north to Quang Tri, the last several months until the end of January '68 was just non-stop action. Every bird available was on active flight status, but unlike our situation at Ky Ha, when there were regularly 10, if not more birds available on a given day, that was not the case at Quang Tri. The attrition rate due to battle damage, and the lack of 24/7 maintenance continued to reduce the number of available birds. Slowly but surely the war was taking its toll on all the squadrons. Frequency of contact with the NVA was increasing daily. I recall the priority for the first available gunship was for the medevac escort (which was one gunship and one transport). Then if there were enough birds to form two sections of gunships (a section was two birds), one section held at the air base on standby, the other section probably sent to Khe Sanh. But if not enough for two sections, they would add a third bird to the first section, and we would either head for Khe Sanh or remain at Quang Tri on standby; but either way, there was no down time if your bird was up and available. And for whatever reason my bird WB#3 was always up, of which I am very proud.

CHAPTER 21

Con Thien Overrun

Another day in December or early January, the squadron only had three gunships available; one bird was on medevac escort, and two of us were on standby at the air base. It was a heavy overcast day about mid-morning when the duty officer came running in the ready hooch screaming very excitedly that he had just received word from Land Shark, "Scramble all available gunships!" Con Thien was under heavy attack and in danger of being overrun. Con Thien was the northwest camp in the Leatherneck Square.

All three crews took off running for our birds, and just as quickly as we were able, got airborne, and then rushed up to Con Thien. Evidently, the NVA had been waiting for the right day with the right conditions for their attack and knew that air support would be mostly unavailable with the overcast sky and the ceiling well under 1,000 feet. Fixed-wing aircraft from Da Nang and/or from aboard navy carriers out on the South China Sea could not help because of the extremely low ceiling, and we three Huey gunships were all that could be mustered.

I don't remember if there was a lead bird, nor who was the senior pilot in command, or which were the chase birds, or if there was one; we just ran for our birds, saddled up and hauled ass north into the DMZ. We arrived over Con Thien maybe 10 minutes after we took off and came upon a crazy chaotic scene. It was impossible to identify Marines from the NVA, we could not tell who was who. The NVA had penetrated the northwest wire and were inside the camp's perimeter. I had no idea who to shoot at, so I just fired every round I could around at the outside of the perimeter.

I don't remember any conversation on the radios between the three gunships, either on our way up to Con Thien or among the crew on my bird, it was so disorganized. The mission was just to get there as fast as possible and try to break up the battle and keep the NVA from overrunning the camp. There had been no time for anyone to develop a strategy, figure out what we were going to do when we got there; it was just pure chaos. Within 10–15 minutes after arriving over the Marine camp, we had expended almost all, if not all, of our rockets and 7.62 ammo. I don't remember, or even know if there was any coherent radio communication between the gunships and Con Thien's command post, or even between the birds after we arrived. Con Thien's camp was not very large, about the same size as the other three Leatherneck outposts; and I would say perhaps the diameter of the camps was about 200 yards, if that large, and it's a wonder that we did not have a midair collision with one another operating in such a small area. But at one point I noticed something next to my bird out of the corner of my right eye, and happened to look out through the gunner's door and saw one of the other birds was very close, too close to us; but then I realized that I was looking only at the top of its rotor head; the bird was falling sideways. I thought for sure the other crew was going down, in the middle of Con Thien. But after a few more minutes, and having expended all our ammunition, it was over, and we were heading back; it was then that I realized that all three of us were still in the air and were returning to Quang Tri. I can't say if we had been responsible for breaking up the NVA attack, but the presence of three gunships overhead must have helped, and Con Thien was still there, and intact; I believe that the three gunships had accomplished our objective.

Another aspect of the above event is the fact that the primary reason for moving the squadrons north to Quang Tri was probably to locate helicopter support as close as possible to Khe Sanh, Leatherneck Square and the Marine outposts; it was clearly obvious that enemy forces and activities were increasing daily. But the underlying fact was that the NVA and the VC situation was also taking its toll on the availability of the helicopter support. Every Marine helicopter squadron at Quang Tri was having difficulty keeping up with the demand for support. The above mission at Con Thien was only a sample of the lack of availability that

VMO-6 was having; only three gunships were initially available. When we got back to the air base it turned out that the other two gunships had also been badly shot up and put out of service; and then for the better part of the next week, my bird WB#3 was the only Huey still available at Quang Tri. And for most of the following week WB#3 and I were on medevac escort missions. VMO-6 was down to one gunship, with no other birds available for other missions, either too much battle damage, or awaiting replacement parts.

Thirty years later at one of our squadron reunions, when we were all sitting around with a beer and drink in hand, telling lies, sharing our war stories, I heard Ed Kufeldt describing the day when he was heading back from Con Thien, flying the only remaining gunship in the squadron that wasn't shot up, and was still up and available. It was only then that I knew that it was Captain Ed Kufeldt who had been my pilot that day over Con Thien.

For the next several days, I remember well that almost all the Medevac missions were 3-4 miles to the north, across the Qua Viet river and in the area east of Highway One and a couple miles from the Marine base camp at Dong Ha, the southeast corner of Leatherneck Square. It appeared that each time the Marines would send out on a patrol in that area, they were ambushed, so we were there several times, several days in a row, and in the same area while escorting a Marine CH-34 picking up wounded Marines.

To describe the area: at the mouth of the Qua Viet river at the South China Sea, on the south side, about a quarter mile from the river, there was a US Marine Amtrac base, and then the provincial town of Quang Tri was a short distance further to the south. The area north of the river was open terrain with nothing but sand and sparsely growing thin pine-like trees. It was hard to understand how, but the local VC were there, living underground, and sniping at the grunts when they ventured out on patrol. It was difficult to tell exact distances while flying, but I'm guessing that from the shoreline of the South China Sea across to Highway One was perhaps several miles. It seemed that every day while I was on medevac standby that week, the Marine patrols out of Dong Ha were ambushed, and/or the VC or NVA snipers would hit them.

On that first day when we were called out to medevac the wounded, our partner, a CH-34, was on the ground picking up WIAs on the north side of the river, while we were down at treetop level scouting the area towards the ocean where the enemy fire had been coming from. Both the gunner and I were up on the door guns, safeties off, ready to shoot, when suddenly as we were over the mouth of the river and about to swing to the north and head back around toward the 34, I caught sight of three VC on the north bank of the river, not 30 yards away from us. Apparently, they saw us coming and had already dropped their weapons in the opening; they were unarmed when I spotted them. We had caught them getting back in at the entrance of their hideaway tunnel system. I yelled "Nine o'clock" to the pilot; he turned to look and came back "Shoot." I opened fire with the door gun, but in a flash, they had disappeared. I'm hoping that I had hit them, or at least wounded them, as the rounds were kicking up sand all around and behind them, but in that instant, they made it back into their tunnel system. We swung back around to the north, then west in the direction of the 34, as they had just called and were waiting for us, ready to lift off with the WIAs.

The next day we were back in the same area, just north of the river and perhaps a mile east of the Dong Ha Marine camp and Highway One, and again, a Marine patrol had been ambushed. And again, with the 34 on the ground picking WIAs, both the gunner and I were up on the guns, safeties off, ready to shoot; this time we were about 100 yards north of the river, zipping along at treetop level going about 120 knots heading back toward the 34. I was scanning the area to the south toward the river, when suddenly I noticed movement directly below us and looked down. There were three Viet Cong running and heading west in the direction of the 34, which was still on the ground waiting for us, maybe a half-mile ahead. The middle one was tall for a Vietnamese, but he was carrying what looked like an anti-aircraft gun, very long, with a flared barrel end. Running at his side was another normal-size man, who was carrying what looked like a base plate for the gun, and on his opposite side a third who was carrying belts of ammo. We were only about 50 feet above ground, and they were right below us, but my door gun will not shoot straight back because of the tail rotor and tail boom, nor down because of the external guns and the rocket pods, so I grabbed the M-16 and laid face down on the floor, aiming back, but we were going too fast to even get off a shot and they were out of sight in seconds.

When I got back up, I immediately reported to the pilot what I saw (three VC, a very long, possibly an anti-aircraft weapon, base plate, and belts of ammo); he radioed the 34 that danger was coming their way, and that they better get out of there. We had been too close to the ground and directly above their heads, but everything happened so fast that it was extremely hard to react. I was hoping that the pilot would have banked to the left and circled back around because these guys were in the open and sitting (or running) ducks. But our priority was to protect the transport helicopter. Two days in a row, in the same area, we had the enemy dead to rights, but they got away. I'll never know for sure, but my guess was that they were the same three VC, on both incidents.

Many years later Bruce Gossar, the brother of one of the VMO-6 ordnance guys, was in Washington DC looking through the archives and squadron after-action reports searching for info about his brother Corporal Gossar who had passed away. Bruce emailed a copy of an entry that stated, "Cpl Greene spotted VC enemy two days in a row." I can absolutely tell you that it was such an understatement; I spotted VC and NVA almost every day when we flew in the DMZ around Leatherneck Square, because they were everywhere in the DMZ.

I have often wondered why the enemy was not spotted more frequently, especially in the sandy flat area north of the Qua Viet river and east of Highway One. There were no good hiding places; it was nothing but several square miles of flat sandy ground with small, narrow spiny trees with few branches. Obviously, the enemy had made underground tunnels and hiding places. But the only thing I can think of was that when they happened to be caught in the open, that they would just stand next to and hug a tree; trying to spot one was like finding a needle in a haystack. But on the other hand, helicopters didn't fly over there very much because there was no need to, there were no friendly forces in the area; it was nothing but barren ground. Plus, I suspect that helicopters would have become easy targets in these wide-open areas, and the enemy would be able to hear and see us coming from a good distance.

But on the other side of Highway One and the railroad tracks, in the area in and around Leatherneck Square, the terrain changed: instead of flat sand, there were dried-up rice paddies and a lot more trees and vegetation that had grown up around the abandoned paddies. And the areas where the four Marine outposts were located was slightly elevated land, perhaps 40–50 feet higher than the rice paddies. The two outposts on the west side of Leatherneck Square, Con Thien and Cam Lo, had about 150 yards of flat land, before the ground started to elevate into the foothills with plenty of vegetation and jungle right up into the mountains.

The other thing I've wondered about is why nobody else in the bird seemed to see what I saw. I swear that I saw a deer, a buck deer standing at the edge of a treeline just west of Cam Lo. Years later and wondering if I had imagined seeing a deer I did research it—yes, there are deer in the jungles of Vietnam. Also of note, in early 1967 a Marine was pulled out of his foxhole and dragged some distance by a tiger in the DMZ; this was also reported in the *Stars and Stripes*.

Regarding "Cpl Greene spotting VC two days in a row," in the DMZ and surrounding area, unless the gunships were diving toward enemy targets on the ground while on a strafing run and/or with rockets, the safest place to be was right down at treetop level, and even lower, zigzagging and flying as fast as we could, flying about 120 knots. But after all these years, I have concluded that what both the pilots were most concerned about was not hitting anything, like a tall tree or sudden ground elevation, and both pilots had to be ready to take the controls in case the other one was hit by the NVA. As for the pilots looking around for the enemy, that was secondary, and probably not a good idea. The gunner doesn't fly as often and might not be used to the breakneck speed and acrobatics that were necessary when we were called for missions in and around Leatherneck Square. But I can tell you for certain, I saw the VC and NVA much more in the last couple of months than my previous time in Nam.

But the fact was that Con Thien and Gio Linh had to be resupplied by helicopter, and their wounded had to be transported out by helicopters. Another factor: not only did helicopters make a lot of noise up in the sky, but they were inviting targets for the NVA when they were heard coming at them from several miles away in the DMZ. Instead of alerting the NVA with the distinctive "wop-wop" of an approaching Huey some distance away, flying right down low at treetop level meant they did not hear the rotor blades, because we would literally jump up on each other. Several times I came face to face with the NVA, who were just as startled as I was, while we were low to the ground, and less than 100 feet away from each other. It was because they were looking up skyward looking for us, they didn't hear us, then in a flash, we had flown past them and out of each other's sight. Flying very low to the ground and coming face to face with the enemy, for the two guys in the back on the side door guns working in the DMZ created a very dangerous and precarious predicament: when to shoot first, and when to hold your fire.

In Vietnam any aircraft flying at a low altitude, under 1,000 feet, were very vulnerable. While I was at Quang Tri, they had moved in a small fleet of fixed-wing one-man aircraft that were used for surveillance missions in the I Corps area. I'm not sure of the military name and/or designation of the planes, but I think they were probably Cessna 0-1 Birddog aircraft, or similar. They were stationed at the north end of the airstrip and may have been incorporated with VMO-6 then, or afterward. I heard that the squadron received more aircraft to supplement the loss of the Hueys, but I'm not sure, as my tour was just about up. But there were a couple times, while I was still there, when the pilot of the "Birddog" aircraft had been hit by ground fire and he barely made it back to the air base. One of those times we were getting ready to taxi out on the airstrip and take off on a mission when the tower or the duty officer came on the radio, to tell us to hold up and wait until the small plane landed; the pilot had been wounded and they didn't know if he could land the aircraft. I'm not sure how badly he had been hit but he was able to make it back to Quang Tri and safely land his plane. The other time we were on standby in the flight hooch at Quang Tri when we got word that the pilot had also been seriously wounded and might not make it back, and/or able to land on the airstrip. All of us were watching from outside the ready hooch, about 50–60 yards away, when he was able to make the landing, I remember that we were all cheering and raising our fists that he was safely on the ground.

The fact was that flying at lower altitudes up in the DMZ or around Khe Sanh was very dangerous, especially for the slower observation aircraft. As previously mentioned, on missions in the DMZ during the later stages of my tour, there were many NVA that I was able to spot. Unless we happen to catch them moving in the open, it was very difficult to see them at normal flying altitude, but down near to the ground it was easy to spot them, but not enough time to react to the situation, as they were looking for aircraft up in the sky.

On a resupply mission with the transport chopper(s) on the ground at either Con Thien or Gio Lin, we were zooming around below treetop level over the rice paddies, when I came face to face with two NVA soldiers. They were in a fox hole, at the base of a tree among the edge of some low-growing vegetation. They were hiding in a fox hole with only the upper portion of their bodies exposed; one was manning his machine gun and the other beside him ready to feed the belts of ammo. Again, they were looking up, looking for us in the sky. I was also up on the door gun, the safety was off and ready to shoot, but for that split second, I was not sure who they were, good guys or NVA, and before I could acclimate myself as to where we were, they were gone and out of sight. There just was not enough time to process the situation, and that was the problem, at least for me. I did not want shoot fellow Marines.

CHAPTER 22

Enemy in the Open

In December '67 or January '68 we were a section of gunships heading back to Quang Tri after a Marine Recon insertion in the area southeast of Khe Sanh, when Land Shark called and directed us to head further north to fly shotgun over a couple of Marine patrols up in the DMZ. We were the lead bird again; my pilot oversaw the section. Land Shark indicated the grunts had an ALO (Air Liaison Officer), a Marine pilot embedded with the Marines on the ground, and to check in with him. We easily found the Marines, as they had already started their patrol out of Gio Linh, which was the northeast corner of Leatherneck Square, and was just a mile or so south of the Ben Hai River which divides North and South Vietnam. There were two columns of grunts, both moving north, one column on Highway One, the other on the old railroad tracks which were about 50–60 yards apart and further inland to the west. The railroad tracks and Highway One run parallel to each other in that area.

As the lead gunship, I remember that our altitude was only about 500 feet so that we could better see ahead of the forwardmost Marines on the "point"; we were positioned between the two columns. The column on the pilot's side was on Highway One which was mostly clear of trees and bushes, but on my side the railroad tracks had heavy growth of foliage on each side; the middle of the railroad bed had 2–3-foot vegetation mostly covering it and presented plenty of opportunities for an ambush. As we were flying north toward the Ben Hai river, I could see the lead elements of the Marine patrol on the railroad tracks, but then looking ahead, I happened to notice another group of two or three people on the tracks a little further north of that column's lead. I came up on the intercom to the pilot that I was pretty certain that I had identified the Marines on the point, the lead elements of the grunts, but looking further ahead there was another group, and I wasn't sure who might be, maybe 40–50 yards north of the grunts' lead element. The pilot immediately banked to the left and descended a bit, so I could get a better look. As soon as he turned, two or three NVA soldiers, who had been lying in ambush, jumped up, dropped their rifles, threw off their helmets and gear, and started running straight back toward North Vietnam. And as they were running several more joined them, also dropping everything, and sprinting as fast as they could to run north to the river.

We had a dream come true—six or eight NVA, obvious new recruits, in the open, running back for North Vietnam. We knew that they were North Vietnamese. The pilot radioed that we had enemy on the run, but the ALO pilot with the grunts was further back in the column, and he would not give us permission to fire until he knew for sure where the grunts in the lead were. Looking down we could see the grunts up on the point shooting at the fleeing NVA, but we were ordered to hold fire. And while we waited for permission, we watched them running up to the old blown-up railroad bridge then jumping and diving off the abutment into the river and swimming back into North Vietnam. After a couple minutes of utter frustration, patiently waiting, and now watching the NVA climbing up the riverbank inside North Vietnam, we received another call from Land Shark. The Recon team we had inserted an hour earlier was now in trouble, and we had to head back and get them out; Land Shark stated that the transport choppers had already been dispatched. And we had no sooner turned around to fly back south, when the ALO came up on the radio and said that he was now up at the point, and we had his permission to fire. But it was too late; the NVA who were lying in the ambush were back in the north.

That would have to be one of the most frustrating days that I had in Vietnam. Had we not been there, I'm certain that those Marines on the ground would have walked a very short distance, and the Marines up on the point would have been cut down. Fortunately, we were available, and Land Shark called for us to ride shotgun over the column. But for most of the previous year while we were on standby, it was the norm for Land Shark to call for the gunships to come to the aid of Marines caught in an ambush way too often, and so many times a Marine transport chopper was badly shot up, or even shot down, while the enemy escaped back in the bush or jungle so that they could spring another future ambush. But that day on the above mission riding shotgun over the Marine patrol out of Gio Linh, it would have been our turn to mete out the punishment on the bad guys. It was a very frustrating day.

CHAPTER 23

No Joy

Another day probably in January '68, we were a section of guns on standby at Khe Sanh, when Land Shark wanted us to help find a downed helicopter crew about 15–20 miles southwest of Khe Sanh. It was one of the same areas of operations that we had frequented when the squadron was working the MACV-SOG missions earlier in the spring and summer. I suspected, but was not sure, that the downed crew must have been US Army, which had taken over the SOG missions for the squadron when we moved north to Quang Tri.

We flew for about 10 minutes to the area where the reported emergency beeper was coming from; it was obviously near the Ho Chi Minh Trail. The area was nothing but hills and mountains with a thick jungle canopy. The whole area west and southwest of Khe Sanh was so ill-defined as far as the border, I have no idea whether we were over Vietnam or Laos. But both of us gunships frantically searched the area, down low, just above the trees searching the green foliage. The beeper was loud and clear, but we could not even find the crash site. There was no sign of the downed helicopter, only the clear audible emergency beeper. I am sure that the other crew members felt the same way, as it could have been any one of us down there trying to survive in the horrific conditions of the Vietnamese jungle, in no man's land, with the NVA searching for the "American imperialists." Such a helpless feeling that we failed to find those guys, or even locate the crash site, and I am certain that we were their only hope of getting out of there alive. But the fact was that it could have been the NVA, that they already found the downed crew, had their emergency beeper, and were hoping to shoot down another helicopter to capture and/or kill four more Americans, but we will never know.

We finally ran out of time, reported to Land Shark "No joy," and had to head back to Khe Sanh. On the way back we were flying at about 800–900 feet over the jungle canopy but flying a little further west toward Laos than our flight path down to the beeper area; it was a good idea not to fly on the same route because of the possibility of the NVA anticipating our return trip back to Khe Sanh and setting up their anti-aircraft guns. And shortly after heading back to Khe Sanh and as we looked over to our left, there was the enemy; a North Vietnamese man operating a bulldozer, in plain sight, perhaps less than a quarter of a mile away. There was no doubt that we saw each other. But seeing two helicopter gunships flying nearby didn't seem to bother him at all, he just kept working the dozer, clearing the trees and jungle and continuing to build the road along the top of a low ridgeline. From the sky, that cleared dirt road behind him looked almost like an interstate highway in the middle of the vast jungles of Vietnam and Laos.

As we flew by, the enemy soldier and dozer appeared to be a little closer so I loaded a grenade in the M-79 and carefully raised the barrel, hoping to get more distance, but also so that the grenade did not hit the end of one of the rotor blades. I fired off the round but it fell well short. Thinking back about that episode now, I wish I would have thought to take a photo of that scene, an NVA and his bulldozer in plain sight, but I'm also sure in our minds, we were all wondering if there was anti-aircraft looking at us. I know that on the way down to look for the downed US Army crew, and on the trip back, there were hundreds, if not thousands of NVA on the ground that caught a quick glimpse of us of us while looking up through the heavy jungle foliage; flying over the areas around the DMZ and Khe Sanh was very dangerous. As we were flying back to Khe Sanh, there was no discussion, no intercom conversation, the situation wasn't even reported to Land Shark. But I'm sure that the veterans among the eight of us knew that the war had changed. I thought how quickly that change had happened: just six months earlier while we were working with the SF SOG teams, and gathering information to try and prove to Congress that North Vietnam was transporting war materials using heavy-duty trucks to the south, we would have attacked that dozer and the operator, or called in a fixed-wing air strike on him, but late in my tour, the NVA had turned the Ho Chi Minh Trail into a major highway and were building it with impunity.

After I rotated home from Nam and discharged from the USMC, and for many years after, I was convinced that during the squadron's SOG era, and even later while we were based at Quang Tri and working the DMZ area, had my bird had been shot down, and they were unable to get us out, we no doubt would have been captured and/or killed by the NVA. Or if somehow we were able to evade capture, we could not have survived in the jungle. Getting back to Khe Sanh would have been next to impossible as there were tens of thousands of NVA crawling around the whole area. Probably heading west was the most realistic option, but even if you were able to evade the NVA there, it was questionable if we would have been able to find any friendlies in Laos because the North Vietnamese were there in large numbers also, and basically controlled the entire area. Without regard to the enemy, the VC or the NVA and being captured, trying to survive in that extremely thick jungle would have been next to impossible. For many years my thoughts were—if we had been shot down, probably we would have perished there. Five months after I rotated back home to the States, it was reported that the Marines abandoned the combat base at Khe Sanh.

Subsequently, 20–25 years after Nam, while I was working on the railroad, I met a "new hire" and a retired career air force officer who turned out to be a good friend. When he found out that I had been in helicopter gunships, he started asking me about my experiences in Vietnam. When I told him about working on the SOG SF missions early in my tour and a lot of work with Marine Recon back in the jungles in and around the foothills and mountains in the western side of the I Corps area, he mentioned that his brother was a retired Navy SEAL, who had gone to work for a private contractor, doing classified work. He also told me that his brother had given him a book, a book that I needed to read. He insisted that I read it and let me borrow it. I did read it and then bought a copy for myself. It's about Vietnam and the POWs and is called *Kiss the Boys Goodbye*, by Monika and William Stevenson. After reading it, I started thinking about that downed US Army gunship crew in late '67 that we failed to find in the area southwest of Khe Sanh, and the NVA bulldozer clearing the road for the extension of truck traffic on the Ho Chi Minh Trail. Had we had gone after the dozer, more than likely we would have been shot down and had the same fate as the army crew. And it was in the same general area that we had the CH-46 with the second Marine Recon team aboard shot down 8–9 months earlier when we were working SOG missions out of Khe Sanh.

After our move to Quang Tri, the squadron was mostly working the northern portion of the I Corps area, the Khe Sanh area and the DMZ, supporting the Marines there. And I am certain the US Army SF had the SOG missions along the rest of the Ho Chi Minh Trail, probably all the way to Saigon. How many of their birds had been shot down? How many of the small Montagnard villages back in the foothills and mountains that had been manned with embedded SF advisors? And how many fixed-wing pilots had been shot down bombing along the trail, not to mention in North Vietnam? I'm not privy to how many Marine Recon teams might have been lost in the DMZ and/or around the Khe Sanh area, even further south in the I Corps area, but I know, as a squadron, we did our best to get them all out. But I can tell you, thinking back to that day out of Khe Sanh while we were hearing the emergency beeper loud and clear, and searching for the US Army helicopter crew on the ground, collectively we all had a very sick feeling that day when we tried but failed to get those guys out of there.

CHAPTER 24

SOG Team in Trouble

Late in my tour, and getting "short," I was in a section of three gunships out of Quang Tri on standby for the day at Khe Sanh. We were the lead; my pilot was senior and in command of the section. Late in the afternoon Land Shark called and directed us to fly southwest, meet up with and escort a pair of Marine CH-34s on an emergency resupply mission for a team on the ground, an area in or near the Ho Chi Minh Trail. During the mission, I concluded that this was not Marine Recon, it must have been a Special Forces team on a SOG mission because the number of people on the ground was much too large for Marine Recon, and too small for a Marine operation out that far away from Khe Sanh. But on that day and that mission, I had no idea about the absence of the army gunships and/or the "King Bee" CH-34 transports, who normally would be supporting the team on the ground. But it had been 4–5 months since the squadron had been relieved of supporting the SOG missions around Khe Sanh, and the US Army choppers had taken over those responsibilities, and the dynamics of the war had probably changed.

When we arrived with the Marine CH-34s at the drop site, it was clear that the guys on the ground were in big trouble, and in a desperate situation: they were surrounded by a larger body of NVA, and they were rapidly running out of ammunition and supplies. The team was holding the top of a small hill amid taller foothills and mountains in the area southwest of Khe Sanh, and they appeared to be surrounded. There looked to have been a lot of explosions on the hill because the top of it was mostly cleared of vegetation, but there were several larger, tall trees still standing, preventing the transport choppers landing in the zone. After arriving, the lead 34 tried to come to a hover overhead at the drop site but was unable to hold steady because of intense enemy fire. Despite the fact of having us three gunships rotating around the small perimeter, and doing everything we could, shooting up and blasting the surrounding area, we could not suppress the heavy enemy fire which was coming at us and the 34s from all sides. The lead 34 could not get close enough to even momentarily hover over the top of the hill to drop any of the much-needed ammo and/or supplies. The 34s were sitting ducks, and finally, the lead 34 pilot indicated that the LZ was too hot, and with that sitrep Land Shark ordered us and the 34s to return to Khe Sanh.

After our return to Khe Sanh, and given the lateness of the hour, Command had to send the shot-up CH-34 transports back to Quang Tri and ordered that we (three gunships) would spend the night and make another attempt to resupply the team at first light. It was surprising to keep us there, because Khe Sanh had become such a magnet for mortar and artillery fire, especially when helicopters were present at night. But clearly the SOG team was in trouble, and we ended up spending the night in the bunker next to Khe Sanh's CP (command post). During our SOG missions, earlier in the summer, there were several times when we had to stay over at Khe Sanh because the SF SOG teams were still on the ground for the night, and they needed us nearby in case the teams got into trouble. Previously when staying over during SOG missions, we stayed in different bunkers near where the regular Marines stationed there stayed. But as been previously mentioned, the war around Khe Sanh, and the DMZ, had increased considerably in the past 5–6 months, and holding the gunships over was a major risk.

Earlier in the evening, Land Shark and Khe Sanh Command conferred with my pilot and reported that the CH-34 transports earlier in the day had sustained too much battle damage and had to return to Quang Tri, and they didn't think that there would be any 34s available first thing in the morning, but that the situation with the team on the ground was desperate. And Command made the request that we attempt the early morning mission and try to make the resupply ourselves. It was decided that the lead gunship would dump half our fuel, and we would carry as many resupplies as we could get aboard the bird, and hopefully still get airborne. Sometime during the night, they loaded up my bird with stacks of munitions and supplies in the space between the gunner and me, which was about four feet high, with no room left to move about.

There were 12 of us (three VMO-6 crews), and it turned out to be very hard indeed trying to sleep that night. Just about everything at Khe Sanh was underground with trench lines connecting the different bunkers. That night the bunker we stayed at was next to Khe Sanh's command post; it was small and there were already several other Marines sacked out trying to sleep. There was only a thin wooden door separating us from all the radio commotion coming from the CP, and all night long, all we heard was the radio traffic coming from the SOG team in the bush, their desperate situation, plus all the other normal activities occurring in and around the Khe Sanh perimeter.

One thing that I must mention, and will never forget, when we opened the door to the bunker where we were to stay, besides the several Marines sleeping there, we also saw the largest rat in the world. It was as large as the biggest, fattest cat I've ever seen. These poor Marines at Khe Sanh had to deal with not only incoming artillery, mortar rounds, and frequent ground attacks, but also those giant rats running around. We had heard that there were plenty of those rats out beyond the perimeters feasting on numerous NVA bodies; and for many reasons, besides the rats, obviously Khe Sanh was not a great place to be stationed. I think I can speak for the 12 of us: it was not a very good night. Certainly not one that I would get used to, or ever forget.

Fortunately for the team on the ground, it was a perfectly clear sky that night, and most of the radio traffic was coming from and about the SOG team. They had air cover overhead, a FAC (forward air controller) up in a small fixed-wing aircraft, and flare planes out of Thailand, with attack jets bombing the surrounding area all night. To say the least, I doubt that any of us got much rest trying to not listen to all the radio chatter going on that night and/or thinking about that monster rat.

The next morning as dawn was starting to break, we had already been up and about keeping busy; we crew chiefs had pre-flighted our birds, and I had dumped half our fuel; the gunners were recleaning the guns and getting ready for the upcoming shit sandwich. Everybody was ready and it was about time to depart, but as I was standing there in front of my bird, holding down the rotor blade from flapping in the wind, waiting for the pilot to give me the cue to release it so he could start the engine, I began to think about how "short" I was (nearing the end of my tour), and started thinking for the first time, now that my 13 months was almost up, that perhaps I was going to make it out of Nam, and maybe go home. I can honestly say that there were only three times that I was nervous in Vietnam. The first time was when I was one of the three FNGs in the Huey slick a year earlier, when the crew chief told us that we were taking fire, and to take off our hard hats and sit on them, as we were about to touch down in the LZ in the middle of a big battle. The second time was a couple months later after the CH-46 and the Recon team had been shot down and we were flying back to Khe Sanh on fumes, wondering if we were going to make it. And the third was standing there holding that rotor blade at Khe Sanh, wondering what my fate might be that day.

I'm sure the other crew chiefs in the squadron felt the same way as I did. I loved having my own bird and doing what we did; we were like a safety net, helping other Marines. But for myself, the only time that I got nervous over there was when I had time to think about what was about to happen. Most of the time, when we were hurrying to get to the Marines on the ground who were in trouble, trying to protect the transports from enemy fire, emergency refueling/rearming etc., everything else was the same emotion: you're on a mission when suddenly you are taking fire so you just react to the situation, you don't have time to think about it. But that morning at Khe Sanh, I had time to think about it.

Just before the sun was coming up over the mountains to the east, we took off and headed south. There was no room between me and the gunner, mostly ammo, grenades, and a couple cases of C-Rations. When we arrived at the SOG team's location the sun was up, and it was full daylight. My pilot radioed to the unit on the ground to pop smoke around their perimeter so that we knew where to shoot, and so he could tell the wind direction when we were hovering over the drop zone. We approached the drop zone from the northeast with the two chase birds covering our six o'clock, both the gunner and I blasting away at the high ground on each side of their perimeter.

The two chase birds started firing rockets and guns at the surrounding jungle outside the perimeter as we came to a hover not far off the ground, just above the few still-standing trees. The gunner kept firing away on his side and I waited for the pilot to settle the bird and hover over the zone, and to cue me when to start unloading the boxes of supplies. I don't know if we were taking fire or not, but when he gave me the nod, I started throwing the cases of supplies out the door. Immediately after the first box of ammo went out the door, the team's radio man on the ground came back on the radio saying that it had almost hit one of their guys below, and that I had to be more careful and try to avoid hitting anyone on the ground.

I wasn't looking for anyone down below on the ground, and there was no doubt that those guys on the ground were in dire need of ammo, and probably didn't have much, or none, and they were desperate to get at it. But what they didn't understand is that a Huey gunship and a CH-34 are not alike; the 34 has an open door where you can hold the cargo out and just drop it straight down. You can't do that with a gunship, as the elevated side outrigging which holds up the external guns and rocket pods extends up and outward about 2 feet from the side of the bird; I had to throw each resupply package out and over the outrigging. The pilot, trying to hold the bird steady in a hover, temporarily looked back and realized what I had to do getting those supplies out the door, then immediately radioed back to the guys on the ground that they needed to back away and wait until all the cargo was on the ground. And I just kept throwing out the supplies as fast as I could. As soon as the last box was finally out, I yelled "All set," and as we were flying away, I jumped on the door gun to cover our retreat. I pulled the trigger and bam, one round, my damn door gun jammed. I grabbed my M-16 and fired, bang, one round, and that jammed too. Amazingly, we didn't take one hit! How could anyone be so lucky? We climbed back up in the sky, mission accomplished, and headed back to Khe Sanh.

Afterward, I concluded that it was likely that most of the NVA must have pulled back. The previous night's clear sky would have allowed heavy airstrikes. I have to believe that the NVA were getting such a pounding all night from the air assault thrown at them that they must have moved back, because the amount of enemy fire was nowhere near what it was that previous day. We returned to Khe Sanh to refuel and rearm; and obviously, I had two weapons to clean. I don't remember if we stayed for the rest of the day there at Khe Sanh, or immediately flew back to Quang Tri, but that was the day I began to realize that I was getting "short" and maybe I would make it back to the world.

In retrospect, immediately afterward and later in life, thinking about the above emergency resupply mission and recalling what the transport squadrons had to do day in day out in Nam for the Marines on the ground, I want to emphasize that during my time in Nam I have gained the utmost respect for all USMC Aviation in Vietnam. Not just for my squadron, VMO-6, but VMO-2 and 3 as well, and the transport squadrons and the flight crews of the CH-53, and especially the CH-34 and 46 squadrons regarding the missions that were been involved with during Nam. Specifically, I am referring to that day at Khe Sanh, holding that rotor blade, wondering if that was going to be my last day on earth; the Marines in the transport squadrons had those same thoughts and emotions practically every day in Nam. Throughout their tours, especially in late 1967 and after the Tet offensive, wondering if that shit sandwich that they were about to head into was the day that they were going to die.

I think back to early in my tour, in April '67, while I was still very inexperienced, when I heard that CH-46 pilot with his southern drawl on the radio: "Klondike, if we are going to get those folks out of there, we have to do it right now, my fuel warning light just came on." He and his crew had been watching from not far away when their fellow 46 partner had been shot down in the ambush with the Recon team aboard. That pilot and his crew were heading into their next shit sandwich, knowing that they had to land 20–30 feet downhill from the burning 46 to get their fellow squadron mates and the Recon team the hell out of there. Was that one of the many, many days that they thought they would die? Those are just a couple of the tens of thousands of rescue missions that all helicopter crews faced every day in Vietnam. And I would remind everyone reading this, regarding that CH-46 with the second Recon team aboard shot down in April '67: it was just one of 12,000 helicopters shot down during Vietnam.

CHAPTER 25

Gio Linh Resupply

Late in my tour and for reasons to be explained later, I was with Captain Ed Kufeldt for day standby at Quang Tri, and that day we had been designated as the chase bird. The lead gunship was piloted by Captain Neff, his co-pilot was Captain Sonny James, the crew chief Corporal Sutton (who was filling in for Corporal Harris) and his bird was WB#20. I don't remember who their gunner was, nor the co-pilot or gunner on my bird that day.

One of our early missions that day, Land Shark had assigned our section a resupply escort mission with two CH-46 transport helicopters at Gio Linh, the northeast corner of Leatherneck Square, in the DMZ. Gio Linh was less than a mile south of the Ben Hai river, separating North and South Vietnam, and a very short distance west of the abandoned railroad tracks and Highway One which ran parallel in a north and south direction. Practically all resupply missions of the Marine outposts in the DMZ at that time were from the air because of the numbers of NVA who operated in the area. Resupply by ground was next to impossible.

At the outset of the mission, the first CH-46 was attempting to land at Gio Linh but was waved off because of enemy ground fire coming from the foliage and brush along the old railroad tracks only a couple hundred yards away to the east. Captain Neff had instructed the CH-46s to climb up and stay out of range while we attacked the enemy position.

To fly into the DMZ to attack the enemy with our machine guns and/ or fire rockets, the gunships had to climb to a less-than-desirable and unsafe elevation, so that the pilots were looking down on the enemy targets.

When at sufficient height, then the pilot would nose the bird downward and start firing while holding the descending dive angle. When the lead gunship pulled away, the chase bird protecting the lead's six o'clock, then started his gun run, and so on.

With the 46 transports up out of range and out of the area, both lead and chase gunships were climbing and jockeying for position for our strafing runs. I'm sure I was not paying particular attention to the altimeter, as we all were watching for enemy fire coming our way, but I would guess that our attack elevation started at about 750–800 feet, and that we would pull out at perhaps 300 feet or so. And as previously mentioned, the most vulnerable position for the gunship was after pulling out of a strafing or rocket run, turning right or left "low and slow," and then climbing back up in the sky with only one single side gun protecting the bird on each side.

Captain Neff, in the lead, indicated that we our strafing runs would go from west to east, starting over the area between Gio Linh and the Con Thien outpost. We would shoot at the area that the enemy fire was coming from along the railroad tracks a little north and east of Gio Linh, then pull out to the south toward Dong Ha. The area west of Con Thien is where the North had hidden their artillery and anti-aircraft weapons, not a good area to start our attack, but this was the DMZ, a very dangerous place. There was no good or ideal area to start a gun run.

I don't recall if Captain Neff elaborated his plan of attack over the radio, but I recall that when we started getting into position heading westerly, then turning 180 toward Gio Linh to start our gun runs, we were nearly over the Ben Hai river, very close to North Vietnam. There was Gio Linh and/or Dong Ha to the south in the event one of us was shot down, which turned out to be a great asset. As was normal procedure, the chase bird (us) was lined behind and would start our strafing run as soon as the lead pulled out. Then the lead rotates back around, gains altitude, and gets in position to cover the chase when we pull out, and so on.

We followed the lead bird about 200–300 yards behind at about 800 feet, still close to being over the river, then turned south. We were still getting into position to cover Neff when he pulled out of his strafing run, then we would start our own. We watched as Captain Neff nosed over his gunship and started firing his four external machine guns. However, Neff had no sooner started firing when it seemed that a major part of the vegetation line along the railroad tracks, just east of Gio Linh, opened up and started shooting back at him with anti-aircraft fire. We had just started to turn to line up behind the lead bird when Captain Kufeldt realized what was happening and started screaming on the radio to Neff: "Pull out, pull out, it's a trap!" But Captain Neff couldn't: he had already committed, and if he had pulled away, he would have exposed the whole left side of his gunship with only the one door gun against all that anti-aircraft fire coming up at him. There was nothing I could do but watch. I remember jumping up in the middle behind the two pilots to get a better view of what was happening. It was broad daylight as we watched a tremendous amount of heavy anti-aircraft fire coming up aimed at the lead gunship. The rounds that had missed the lead were then flying by us; red, green, and orange tracer rounds.

Looking at a Huey head-on does not give much of a target, but the NVA anti-aircraft fire was hitting the front of Neff's bird and doing damage, and those bullets that had missed the lead bird were then flying past us, over, under, and on both sides of our bird. I especially remember those orange tracer rounds; they looked like orange softballs flying by us. The onslaught reminded me of what a Japanese Kamikaze pilot must have been looking at when he was trying to crash into one of our carriers in World War II.

Captain Kufeldt realized that he could not wait for Neff to turn away, and had to jockey to a different attack position, so he immediately dropped the bird down about 100 feet from our descending attack path directly behind Neff and crew, then swung over to a seven o'clock position behind the lead gunship, and immediately started firing to the left of and past Captain Neff's bird with our external machine guns. At that point the situation was surreal. I have never seen, nor heard of in the Vietnam War, the enemy on the ground shooting right back at two attacking gunships head-to-head. But there we were, two Huey gunships each with four M-60s, eight machine guns firing simultaneously against what seemed like major anti-aircraft rounds coming right back at both of us.

Eight M-60s and 4,000 rounds a minute being fired, all concentrated on the NVA positions; but there was just as much or more coming right back at us, and the NVA were winning.

I remember Captain Kufeldt yelled aloud to the co-pilot, not wanting to take his finger off the trigger on the cyclic stick, to be ready to switch to rockets. Seconds later Captain Neff didn't have a choice as they were closing fast on the NVA, and he had to turn away to the south. As soon as he was out of the way, Captain Kufeldt screamed "Rockets," and the instant the lead bird cleared, Kufeldt fired 14 high-explosive rockets in the NVA positions. As soon as all our rockets were away, we also turned south to follow the lead bird; I emptied the 100 rounds of my door gun into the remnants of the enemy fire; but the rockets had won that battle, there was no more enemy fire coming at us. We followed Captain Neff, who managed to make it down to Dong Ha where they were able to land after taking major battle damage. Amazingly Captain Neff was not hit, but his co-pilot, Captain James, had taken a .50 cal round in his chest and was seriously injured; thank God for bullet bouncers, Captain James survived. After making sure that the other crew was safely on the ground, we continued to Quang Tri and, though I don't recall anything about where nor what we did the rest of the day.

Later, at the end of our day, they had gotten Captain Neff, Crew Chief Sutton, and the gunner back to Quang Tri; Captain James was hospitalized with probably broken bones in his chest, I'm not sure of his status or if his time in Nam was over. But that night I was able to find and spoke with a still-shaken-up Corporal Sutton. He told me that he couldn't believe how many tracer rounds were coming up at them, or how many were hitting the bird, and when they finally were able to turn away, all he could do was to bury his face in his left arm while he continued to fire his door gun with his right hand, because he did not dare to look at all the incoming rounds.

It was the next day when they got the lead bird (WB#20) back to Quang Tri. In addition to numerous bullet holes in the front of the bird, when Captain Neff finally turned south away from the NVA, the whole left side of the helicopter was exposed and the NVA bullets were still coming at them because there were numerous rounds that hit on both sides of Corporal Sutton, and even on the overhead door frame where Sutton was sitting. Corporal Sutton was indeed fortunate not to have been hit or killed. In the front of WB#20 there were numerous bullet holes in both the chin bubbles in front of the pilots, and additional holes elsewhere in the front. The crew of WB#20 were very lucky that Captain Kufeldt was able to get off those rockets that took out the NVA.

There was no doubt in my mind that had it not been for Captain Kufeldt's actions that day the crew of WB#20 would not have survived the heavy onslaught of anti-aircraft fire; it was also very clear that the NVA heavy guns were still firing when Neff pulled away. Without a doubt, it was Captain Kufeldt's flying skills and accuracy with those external guns and then the rockets that determined the fate of Captain Neff and his crew, and for that matter, probably us in the chase bird as well; but it was the 14 high-explosive rockets that took out the anti-aircraft fire.

Later one evening, after getting back from that day's activities. and a couple of days after the above mission, I went to see the CO, Lieutenant Colonel White, as I was wondering if he was aware of the details of the above mission. I told him about what had happened with Captains Neff and James and crew, and of Captain Kufeldt's actions that day. I asked if any of the other pilots had brought it up or reported to him what had happened. He replied that there had been no mention of it from anyone, except from me. So, with Lieutenant Colonel White's reply that no one else had said anything, I told him about what I saw, and what I have written above, and that I believed Captain Neff and crew, as well as us in the chase bird, were probably going down in the DMZ, and probably would have died, if not for Captain Kufeldt and his actions that day. Lieutenant Colonel White responded, "Good, write it up," and said he would take care of it.

Unfortunately, responding to his request/order didn't happen. My only excuse was that I was flying every day. During most of that time the squadron had only two or three birds available; one bird was medevac, and the others off to Khe Sanh. As previously mentioned during the last couple months of my tour, and I am not sure why, other than pure luck, but my bird was always up, and I must admit it was not because of my mechanical expertise. I was just lucky, and just had no time to write the report that Lieutenant Colonel White had asked for. If we (my bird and I) were not on medevac escort, or if there were two or more birds available, then we were sent up to Khe Sanh for the day. At the end of the day when we returned to Quang Tri, it was lights out. Everyone else in camp, who wasn't flying, was working on getting the birds back up and available for service; or building up the sandbags around their hooches or bunkers; there just was no time. Having one of the very few Hueys that was still "up" and available for service, my daily activities just didn't allow me to even think about writing up a report about that day with Captain Kufeldt.

Over 50 years later, thinking about that day over Gio Linh with Captain Kufeldt, I wonder what those Marines on the ground—those who were stationed at Gio Linh, and the other Leatherneck Square outposts—must have been thinking as they watched the fireworks. There they were sitting there in their fox holes or the trench lines that circle the perimeter around Gio Linh, waiting to be resupplied with food and war materials, having front-row seats watching a major event with heavy anti-aircraft fire aimed at two gunships, and the massive amount of enemy firepower only about a quarter of a mile away from their encampment. And watching an unreal show of two Marine gunships firing back and spreading thousands of 7.62 empty brass casings raining down over their heads. But just like Khe Sanh, Leatherneck Square, especially Gio Linh and Con Thien, were dug in in defensive positions and surrounded by the NVA; their only means of resupply and medevac missions was by helicopter. Not to mention that the NVA could and did fire artillery rounds at them every day.

After I got back to the world and for many years afterward, not following up on Lieutenant Colonel White's request to write up that day over Gio Linh bothered me. It was one of my very few regrets in Nam. There are only a couple of those missions that I do remember the names of the pilots; but one of them was Captain Ed Kufeldt. How could I forget his name under those circumstances? And how I didn't follow up with Lieutenant Colonel White. For 30 years after Vietnam, it haunted me that I had not, and I lamented about it many times after I rotated back home.

Several years after Vietnam, I joined the Veterans of Foreign Wars (VFW), and in one of their monthly magazines there was an article about the "Khe Sanh Veterans Association." They were looking for veterans who had been at Khe Sanh; I subsequently joined their organization. In the fall of 1997, I received a directory of their members, and as I was looking through the membership list, that was when I came across Ed Kufeldt's name and address. And with that, I decided to write Ed a letter describing my observation of what had happened that day in the DMZ, and my visit with Lieutenant Colonel White a couple of nights afterward. And my failure to follow up on his request to write it up. It turned out that Ed and now Lieutenant General White (retired) were still friends, and both lived in the same general area in Virginia, and Ed gave me Gen. White's mailing address. I wrote another letter to Lieutenant General White, included a copy of the letter that I had written to Ed Kufeldt and apologized to Gen. White for not getting back to him in January '68.

I really didn't think there would be anything that could be done about it after all the time that had passed, but several weeks later and much to my surprise, General White decided to correct my inaction of 30 years earlier, and he started looking through the old squadron records, and the after-action reports to reacquaint himself with those missions back in 1967–68. Then he contacted Headquarters Marine Corps, and, to make a long story short, in 1999 the USMC presented Colonel Ed Kufeldt (retired) with his second Distinguished Flying Cross. My wife, Kathy, and I were invited to attend the award ceremony in DC, but we did not attend. I was not looking for recognition, but only to relieve my guilty conscience.

During all this time, and since reconnecting with Ed and Bill White, I also discovered that then Lieutenant Colonel White had been wounded a short time later after I departed Nam, and that he lost an eye in a mortar attack at Phu Bai, while waiting for his ride back to the world.

CHAPTER 26

Leaving Vietnam

My 13-month tour was over before I realized it. I have learned in life that keeping busy certainly seems to make time go by fast, and that was certainly the case for me in Nam. I have always liked staying busy, and I am an old man now. I know for a fact that the Good Lord above has been watching over me, I've been lucky all my life and I can offer no complaints. I am so glad and proud that I ended up being a crew chief, and in VMO-6, and am still of sound mind and body, at least I think so.

Believe it or not, I didn't realize that I was getting that "short," not until that day up at Khe Sanh holding that rotor blade, getting ready to take off and attempt to resupply the SOG team which was surrounded by NVA; my tour was over before I knew it. I do remember that late in December or early January, two of our pilots had come to me in the flight hooch while on standby at Quang Tri and asked if I would to extend my tour for six months. They mentioned that I would be given an extra 30-day leave with a round-trip flight to anywhere in the world that I wanted to go, in exchange for signing on for another six months; but I declined, I had had enough. Plus, my family situation back home in the States was concerning.

About the same time that the two pilots had approached me to extend, the squadron had assigned me my "first mec" (jet engine mechanic), another FNG; he would soon be my replacement, and the new crew chief on WB#3, and I don't even remember his name. I was away every day, primarily to Khe Sanh, then not getting back to the air base until late in the day and then it was lights out. But as it turned out with my FNG, it was very similar to the same scenario when I had first arrived in the squadron at Ky Ha a year earlier; I was the FNG and assigned to my crew chief, Sergeant Johnson. I didn't get to see very much of Sergeant Johnson either, nor did I have much opportunity to talk with him, nor get to know him, because he was off flying every day.

Shortly after the two pilots approached me about re-upping for six months, my section leader Sergeant Sherrill and another SNCO came up to me during my morning pre-flight inspection and asked if I wanted to be promoted to the rank of sergeant or given the Navy Achievement Award. I told them that I didn't care. In the end, the squadron decided to award me the Navy Achievement Award with a combat V.

The day I left Vietnam was January 29, 1968. It was early morning, and we (WB#3 and I) were a half of a section of guns. We had already taxied out to the runway to head for Khe Sanh for the day when the duty officer at Klondike Base called on the radio and told the pilot, "Tell Greene to get off, his orders just came in, he's going home." Honestly, I was surprised by the announcement; I knew I was "short," but not that short. But the fact was, I had lost track of time those last couple months in Nam and time had become just a blur. And I just couldn't believe that my Vietnam tour was over. I was both happy and sad at the same time, because my time sitting in the back on the left side of my bird was over. And so was having one of the best jobs in the Vietnam war.

It is difficult to describe that situation of January 29, 1968, but I got out of the bird in a flash and stood there in a stupor, watching my FNG running toward us. After a few moments, I took off my flight helmet, unstrapped my belt with K-Bar knife and holster with my .38 and handed them to him; it was his bird now. The only thing that I do remember, and made sure of, was to grab my camera. After the long walk back and when I got to the ready hooch, I was told to grab whatever personal items I could because within the hour, I had to be on a helicopter heading south for Da Nang. That same afternoon I was on a plane and heading back for Okinawa. I'm sure that the squadron operations anticipated that I was going to extend my tour six more months, because I was a week over the 13-month tour. But what we didn't know at that time was that the Tet Offensive had already started. However, there had been no time to say "Goodbye, good luck" to anyone. There was no time to even turn in the weapons, or other gear that I had checked out and was supposedly responsible for; the FNG inherited everything.

Thinking back to those last days in Nam, it is clear how things had drastically changed for the squadron, and the war. When we were the FNGs at Ky Ha, we had the chance to get acclimated to the squadron and several weeks to start flying as a gunner, and to learn what was going on in this new and strange environment that is called war. Those last two months in VMO-6 there were only three or four gunships "up" and available, whereas a year earlier back at Ky Ha, there were 10 or more birds ready to go, and plenty of opportunity for the FNGs to be assigned as a gunner. Even the pilots, whether new or veterans, were limited for flight time when there so few birds available. How did my FNG get any experience as a gunner? He wasn't the only FNG who needed more on-the-job training in the air and exposure to the enemy shooting at them on just about every mission that they were going to be on. But there he was on January 29, 1968 running out to the take-off strip, taking my place as the crew chief and heading to Khe Sanh.

As I was en route back to the States, my friend Sloop John B, who enlisted with me, was on leave, then on his way to Nam. He had continued in avionics, and then was sent to VMO-1 in New River, NC. We had been able to write back and forth early on when I got to Nam, but when I started flying there was not a lot of time to keep in touch. John departed the west coast on January 27, 1968, arrived in Vietnam in February '68 and was then assigned to VMO-2 at Marble Mountain in Da Nang. He was an avionic technician and he immediately requested to fly as a gunner on their daily gunship assignments. And he got his wish. His letters indicated that he really liked flying, and I understood exactly what he was talking about: I had those same feelings during my time there. We exchanged letters frequently when I got home. He let me know about the missions that he had been on and the NVA offensive and the daily enemy rocket and mortar attacks that were occurring in the Da Nang area, and how often they spent time in their bunkers at night. Unfortunately, six months later, on August 27, Sloop John B's gunship was shot down, and only the co-pilot survived.

In September 1968, one of my friends in Kentucky called to let me know that John had been killed, and that his funeral was in two days. I immediately drove to Boston and caught a flight to Cincinnati. There was a huge crowd at his funeral at St. Joseph Catholic Church, Cold Spring, Ky; when the Mass was over the burial service was in the cemetery next to the church. All throughout the Mass and at the burial service I was doing well, holding back emotions, up and until the Marine officer handed the folded US flag to John's father, Ben Becker. I have been to funerals before, and I have seen dead Marines, squadron members; but when that Marine handed Mr. Becker that flag, and I saw his and Mrs. Becker's reaction, I couldn't hold it back any longer. I immediately hurried away from the crowd and down over a nearby hill, to be by myself so no one would see me all choked up and crying; a big bad Marine, bawling like a baby. One of my best friends, Darlene, came running after me, trying to console me, but I made a fool of myself. I have since apologized to her. She said she understood.

John Becker, died August 27, 1968.

Lieutenant William Vonderhaar.

Our friend Bill Vonderhaar was the first to know what he wanted to do after school: he wanted to be a USMC officer. After high school he enrolled at the University of Kentucky. He enlisted into the USMC on May 13, 1968, the same day he graduated from UK, despite all the anti-war sentiment that was prevalent on college campuses. For six months he was stationed at Officer Candidate School at Quantico, Va, and was promoted to a Second Lieutenant; then he volunteered for Vietnam, and assigned as an infantry officer which was his choice. He arrived in February 1969, over a year after I left. He was sent to An Hoa, the headquarters of the 5th Marine Regiment of the 1st Marine Division. At 24 years of age, he was the CO of 2/5, with 40 Marines under his control.

During an operation in the bush, and setting up for the night, Bill and two others were checking on another platoon that might have been lost, when they happened upon and triggered a booby trap. The two Marines with him were killed and Bill was badly injured in both legs. He was medevaced out to the area aid station, then flown on to the USS *Sanctuary* hospital ship, where he had several surgeries over the next two days to stop the bleeding and remove shrapnel. Then he was flown to Guam for more surgery. At that point both legs were placed in casts and he was flown to Great Lakes Naval Hospital for more surgeries to try and save his legs. Two months later and after more surgeries, they could not save his left leg. In his own words:

> I am not bitter by any of my experiences and viewed most situations as another challenge. I felt that what had happened to me helped me find a career path and finding a wife and three great sons. We were married in March 1971 while I was pursuing a master's degree in Rehabilitation Counselling at the Univ. of Missouri in Columbia, Missouri; we were married on campus. Afterward I worked for the state of Maryland, in Baltimore as a Vocational Rehabilitation Counsellor. We moved to Tucson, Arizona in the fall of 1974, where I completed a Ph. D. program in Psychology, then found employment with the Veterans Administration for 5½ years. In 1979, I was appointed as one of six Regional Coordinators for a newly established program called Vietnam Veterans Readjustment Counselling Program. I left the VA in 1983 for private practice.

Bill met his wife Bev at the VA Hospital in Missouri; Bev was a volunteer for the Red Cross and would come around several evenings after her day job to talk to and console the different vets. They started seeing each other and then started dating after several months when he could get day or weekend passes.

> At first, I think her parents thought that she was just spending time with me because she pitied me, but we have been together for 52 years. Many things happened during my time there but how I exited from Vietnam was so memorable that I can recall it in detail nearly 54 years later. My exit from Vietnam happened in a very disappointing, abrupt, and life-changing manner. However, in retrospect, I have no regrets about enlisting in the Marine Corps or volunteering for Vietnam as my subsequent life unfolded in finding my eventual career path and finding a beautiful and wonderful woman with whom we have had three great sons. It is as if I don't deserve how life took such a fortuitous and favorable twist.

CHAPTER 27

Back Home in the States

I departed Quang Tri about 0800, and then Vietnam mid-afternoon, and arrived in Okinawa later that night, and the following morning they immediately started processing me for my orders back to the States. During the next couple of days, they gave me back my duffle bag with my dress uniforms, refitted me with my winter dress uniform and upgraded my ribbons and some of the medals that I had accumulated over the past 13 months. We departed Okinawa on a commercial airline and flew to Travis Air Base in the San Francisco area. From there I boarded a bus which took me to the San Francisco Airport.

Arriving outside at the terminal area, I was greeted by a young hippie girl and when she saw my medals she shouted, "How does it feel to be a baby killer?" and something else derogatory, which I don't remember. I just ignored her and kept walking. Once inside the terminal I was approached by two Marines, a captain and a sergeant, who were scrutinizing my medals, then asked to see my records and orders. After they were satisfied, I was on my way. My flights were San Francisco to Boston, then on to Presque Isle, in northern Maine. I was greeted there by my mother and her cousin just before midnight. It was about 2am when I finally got to Monticello.

It was early that next morning when I first heard of the North Vietnamese Tet Offensive; the national news media was going crazy about the Tet Offensive. I had been in the States for only a day and a half and knew that the guys back in the squadron were catching hell, as we had been for several months prior; it was a very difficult situation for me.

Half of me wanted to call Headquarters Marine Corps to change my orders, and the other half was looking at my mother and six kids who were living in a rented farmhouse in very rural Maine. My two brothers Tim and Kim were still in high school, and the four Torrey brothers and sisters were much younger. John and Mark were in early middle school, Cathi and Missy even younger.

After arriving home, I bought a car with the money that I had saved for the past 13 months, a later-model Pontiac Lemans 326 sports coupe. After visiting family and relatives in Maine, I drove to Kentucky for a couple days to see my friends there that I grew up with, then continued to NC and VMO-1 at New River. When I arrived at New River Air Station, it was there that I found out about two events in Nam and my old squadron just a few days after I rotated home that really bothered me.

The most disturbing to me was hearing about the loss of Captain Galbreath, Harry Schneider and their crew in mid-February. Before I heard about that, I found out that the NVA had introduced armored tanks into the war—I remembered the NVA who was operating the bulldozer and building the road along the Ho Chi Minh Trail, near Khe Sanh. And then, only a few days after I rotated home, the Special Forces camp at Lang Vei near Khe Sanh had been overrun by the NVA, and the attack was led by tanks. Lang Vei was just a few miles southwest of Khe Sanh, and hundreds of NVA had overrun the camp with the aid of armored tanks. As was the routine when I was still there, the squadron had a section of gunships stationed daily at Khe Sanh, and on that day the gunships spent most of the day supporting the CH-46s which were evacuating the SF soldiers and the friendlies from their camp and the nearby Montagnard village. Reports indicated that many of the Montagnard villagers scattered into the surrounding hills and mountains over the border into Laos or made their way on foot to Khe Sanh. But with tanks and large numbers of NVA inside the perimeter of the SF camp, it was another shit sandwich for the helicopter crews that rescued many of the survivors. Marine CH-46s and 34s and Hueys from the Quang Tri base helped evacuate most of the SF and the Montagnard civilians from Lang Vei, but there were several others who could not get out on the last 34 chopper that lifted out of the camp.

Supported by the VMO-6 gunships, the CH-34s and 46s made numerous trips in and out Lang Vei to rescue the remaining SF guys and local Montagnard but sustained major battle damage from very heavy enemy fire. Then soon afterward came word that there was one more American still in the compound, and another VMO-6 gunship attempted to make the last-minute rescue but was driven away by the massive NVA ground fire.

Many years later, after my wife and I started attending the Pop-A-Smoke and our squadron mini-reunions, I was able to meet up again with Ed Kufeldt and he briefly mentioned to me the Lang Vei mission, but not a lot of the details. But in October 2023, at our Pensacola reunion, I was able to get together again with both Ed Kufeldt and Bob Crutcher; they were the pilot and the crew chief on the attempted rescue of the remaining SF soldier at Lang Vei. I asked them if they would write up what happened that day. The following story is combination of the written summaries that Ed and Bob gave me to describe what happened in that event.

> When word came at Khe Sanh that there was another SF soldier still at the camp, Capt. Kufeldt decided that they had enough fuel left for one last trip, and asked the crew what they thought; Crew Chief Crutcher stated that they had only received small arms fire and that there was an American Green Beret back at Lang Vei who needed help, Lt. Rosental and Gunner Thorton agreed, and the crew headed back toward Lang Vei. Minutes later they arrived over SF camp.
>
> The Air Control pilot reported that he was also low on fuel and had to leave, but before he left, Capt. Kufeldt told him to relay to the Green Beret; there were two WWII Sky Raiders over head with napalm bombs aboard. The plan was to make three runs with their ordnance along the road next to the camp. They were to make two passes dropping the napalm, and on the third run they were to make the same pass, except it would be a dry run, and when they did the third run, the American was to run to the middle of the road at the same time, and they would land and pick him up.
>
> Unfortunately, well made plans don't always work out. As the gunship went in and started to land all hell broke loose. They received small arms fire from their left and later found out from underneath their helicopter. When they tried to land the ground fire was so intense that the bird took over 30 hits, and then the Huey's caution panel lit up like a Christmas tree, and then the engine fire light came on. And immediately smells of jet fuel and hydraulic oil filled the aircraft. Lt. Rosental in the left seat was immediately hit in the arm and his

leg, one of the rounds had hit an artery. He passed out and both Kufeldt and Crutcher thought he was dead. Crutcher was trying to get him out of his seat, as well as busy on his door gun, and he was also hit in the leg, but didn't know it until they got back to Khe Sanh. There was nothing more they could do but abort the mission and try to get to back up in the air and back to Khe Sanh. Miraculously, Capt. Kufeldt was able to pull out of the camp and got airborne. Crew Chief Crutcher was out on the rear of the skid on his side of the bird trying to check on an engine fire, but fortunately there was none.

Kufeldt called Khe Sanh tower and reported that they were on the way back for an emergency landing, and that they might not make it to the base. On the way back the engine started making sounds on two occasions like it was shutting down, but fortunately it did not. He mentioned the Lt. Rosental's flight suit was covered with blood and he thought he was dead. The fire crews pulled the emergency door handle to get him out, and with the immediate attention of the Navy corpsmen, Lt. Rosental survived. But other than being wounded in his leg, Crew Chief Crutcher's biggest lament was that his bird WB#9, Serial #151281, was so badly shot up that it didn't fly again. A couple days later, they sent a CH-53 to Khe Sanh to airlift it back to Quang Tri, but something went wrong en route, the cable holding WB# 9 under the 53 came loose and it fell into the jungle.

It was late February '68 when I arrived at VMO-1, my new duty station; however, there wasn't a whole lot for me to do. I was a corporal and an experienced crew chief, and subsequently there were several times when I would go up on a training flight with a new pilot, but nothing important. Totally different from what we were doing in Nam for the past year. And I don't remember too many new mechanics training to be crew chiefs; I suspect that they were rushed overseas the same as we were. One of my last memories while at New River was playing chess with another corporal, also a Vietnam vet. But as soon as I could when off duty, I was heading for the gym to play round-ball. I found out the squadron had a basketball team, and fortunately for me, the leading scorer on the team at that time was a captain (Captain Pena, I believe that was his name); he was a pilot and sent to Nam a couple days before I arrived. Lucky for me, I took his place on the team, and we ended up winning the New River base championship.

While I was on leave back home in Maine that February, my mother's brother, Roger Hare (Uncle Bud), mentioned that he was going to contact one of our Maine Congressional Representatives to see what could be done about my status. At the time I really didn't think much of it, as I still had a year and half to go on my enlistment. But three months later, at the end of April '68, I received notice from the USMC that I was being "Discharged, under Honourable Conditions" because of my family situation at home. It was not my idea, nor was working in northern Maine, where work opportunities were nil; about the only industry was farming potatoes or working in the woods. But there I was about a week later (in May of 1968) working in a potato house and driving a tractor in the fields.

Prior to being discharged, and on my way south to NC and my next duty station, I had stopped in Portland to visit Uncle Bud and his family, and that's where I met my future wife (Kathy). We started dating shortly after my discharge. I tried to find work in Houlton but couldn't even get a job as a bank teller. One of Mom's relatives, Aunt Chavala, suggested that I apply for the Maine State Police, which I did. But their academy didn't start for another year and half. But as luck would have it, Kathy had two uncles who worked on the Maine Central Railroad, and one of them was a Portland terminal supervisor. Her Uncle Reggie was able to get me hired on the railroad in July 1968. The drawback was that I was the bottom man on the seniority roster, and was subject to being laid off frequently, and the distance between Monticello and Portland is 250 miles, but I was able to stay at Uncle Bud's place briefly, then got a room in Portland for a while.

Two months after I was discharged, my brother Tim graduated from high school and immediately enlisted in the USMC. As soon as he graduated from boot camp and ITR, he was sent to Vietnam, and was stationed in Da Nang. A year later Kim also graduated, also enlisted in the USMC, and afterward was sent to Beauford, NC, Marine Air Base, where he became a crew chief on a Harrier Jet.

In 1970 my older brothers and I were able to save enough to help buy my mother a two-story house in Houlton, Maine. A couple years later she remarried for the third time. With the family situation up in northern Maine resolved, it allowed me to live somewhat of my own life. And a couple of years afterward, Kathy and I were married, and we have lived in Buxton, Maine since. After 30 years on the railroad,

I was able to retire in 2005. After the girls graduated from high school, every November, our anniversary month, Kathy, and I would go on vacation, and eventually were able to travel the entire country, and to visit every state. Kathy died of glioblastoma brain cancer nine years ago. We were married for 46 years, have two daughters, Amanda and Pam, and six grandkids. The Good Lord has always been good to me, in my youth, during Vietnam, and to the present day. I have no complaints; I have been blessed.

CHAPTER 28

Reunions and Reflections

It never occurred to me until much later in life that while in Nam, I don't think many of our squadron mates had much of a chance to really get to know each other, specifically the crew chiefs. Unlike the Marine grunts and the Recon teams who probably spent most, if not all their tours, in the same company, platoon and/or squad on a day-to-day basis; that wasn't the case with the flight crews.

While the other guys in the squadron were generally working together daily, as in the avionics shop, the ordnance guys, the tin knockers, even the SNCOs, they all had mostly daily contact with each other; then, if they wanted to fly as a gunner, they would be away from the shop for just a day or so. The crew chiefs were divided into four sections, one and two in one hooch, three and four in another. If your bird was up and available, then we were always on day standby, or away during the day at an outlying point. At the end of the day, and/or back from TAD assignments, while the rest of the crew dispersed in different directions and headed back to their living quarters and the guys who they work with every day, the crew chief's duties did not end until everything related to his bird had been taken care of. The crew chief was married to his bird. If something had to be corrected or repaired on the bird, we were busy fixing it. Getting to the mess hall, or back to the hooch afterwards, was secondary; there just wasn't a lot of time to socialize.

It was afterwards, many years later, when some of us started getting together at the Pop-A-Smoke reunions, and/or at our VMO-6 mini-reunions, that we really got to know each other. At the reunions, each of the different squadrons had their own separate reunion hooch, and many, many years later, it was then that we really started to communicate with each other and began to bond in a brotherhood. Many of the events of the past in Nam have come to life when the VMO-6 guys started sharing stories and memories.

In the years since Vietnam, I have often wondered about what had happened to many of my squadron mates from VMO-6. Most, we will never find out about, as too much time has passed, but because of the reunions and VMO-6 mini-reunions there are a few that I have reunited with, and we have become very good friends. It was after I got back in touch with Ed Kufeldt, that he mentioned the Pop-A-Smoke reunions and that the next one was coming up in a couple months at Pensacola, Florida, and suggested that Kathy and I should attend. It would be our first of several reunions that we attended. And as luck would have it, our daughter Pam and her husband Mark (both in the USMC) were also stationed there at Pensacola, as Mark had recently graduated from OCS, and was in flight training to be a CH-46 pilot.

When we arrived at the reunion, I really didn't know what to expect; it had been 30-plus years since I had seen, or even heard from anyone in the squadron. But it turned out to be very much what I needed. It was a very big occasion, all the Vietnam-era Marine helicopter squadrons were there, and each squadron had its own tents out on the white sandy beach on the ocean front, and their own hospitality rooms in the hotel. The afternoon when we arrived, of course Kathy didn't know anybody, nor had I seen anyone from Nam in over 30 years. After checking in and as we walked through the hotel lobby, there were numerous squadron members with wives socializing, but almost immediately Ed and I seemed to recognize each other, and finally we met again after all that time. For most of the folks there, I had no idea who they were; many were in Nam before I arrived, some during my tour, and many after I rotated home. We had to read name tags to know who was who. Later that night on the beach, Kathy and I were sitting at a long table full of strangers in our squadron tent, and the white sand reminded me of the sand at the air base at Quang Tri. As I started looking at name tags and trying to recognize someone's name that I might remember, there sitting next to us, suddenly I saw a name that I recognized: Mike Levanduski, the same Corporal Levanduski who I last saw on December 15, 1967 on the ground after the mortar attack at Quang Tri. (He had been lying next to Cpl Evans, both very severely wounded.) Surprisingly, sitting there in the tent at Pensacola, having recovered from numerous major injuries, was Mike Levanduski and his wife Rose. Mike has a full head of white hair, not dark as it was back in 1967, and a heavy white beard. He introduced us to Rose, and they began telling us about the ordeal that he had had since that night in Nam. Without going into too much detail, he obviously had recovered from his open chest and head wounds, but after many difficult operations, the navy doctors had to take one of his ribs and reconstruct a new jaw. He had spent many months, if not years in the hospital. He did not know anything about how Corporal Evans turned out; he had been hit just as bad, but apparently, he also lived, as he is not listed on the squadron KIA list. In the end, Kathy and I enjoyed several more reunions with Mike and Rose, but unfortunately Mike passed away about two years ago.

Regarding General White, I was able to personally meet him again at our VMO-6 memorial ceremony at the Marine Corps Museum in 2006; we didn't get to converse all that much as he was one of several high-ranking USMC generals also in attendance and they drew a lot of attention. He did say that he wanted to chat and thanked me for writing to him, and he told me, no more calling him "Sir," and to call him just "Bill." Sadly, General White is no longer with us. I was hoping that he would have been able to read this so that I could thank him again for making good my mistake 50-plus years ago. But that's what General White, and General Maloney and Colonel Nelson, and numerous other pilots of VMO-6 were all about: superb leadership. Also, I wish I could have finished this sooner because I have mentioned Crew Chief Corporal Pete Harris several times during our SOG, and other everyday missions. Pete and I were among the four or five Marines in the jet engine class together when we got pulled out early and sent to Nam. And we also chummed around together in San Francisco while we were waiting for our orders to head to Nam. Pete was a regular on the SOG missions, but he also passed away several months ago.

Last year, October 2023, VMO-6 celebrated probably our final reunion at Pensacola, Florida: we had a good turnout and had a great time, and I got to see several faces that I hadn't seen for over 50 years. I truly miss seeing some of my very good Marine friends who have passed in recent years.

For over half a century I have always felt how fortunate that I was to have ended up in VMO-6 and to have been one of the crew chiefs. I know for sure that we had something special, the squadron was special. As I have mentioned earlier, there is no question that each of us in the squadron had a hand with our performance of duty, we were the supporting cast and we did it well, but the reality is that it was the pilots that made the squadron. Several years ago, at one of our reunions, I discovered what an understatement that is; and I know that I am not able to acknowledge all the pilots who started in VMO-6 and continued their careers in the USMC, those pilots who rose through the ranks and were promoted to colonel, and even higher. Just a few that come to mind: Captain Kufeldt, Captain Dave Ballantine, who achieved the rank of colonel, and Corporal Arthur Friend (also known as Alfa Golf), who enlisted and designated as a crew chief then was promoted to the rank of lieutenant colonel. I sincerely apologize for those who I am forgetting, or unaware of, but unfortunately, we are all getting old, including yours truly.

In addition, and this is astonishing, I was shocked to learn that our little squadron of VMO-6, with a guesstimate of as few as 150 Marines at any given time over the years of service in war, have had at least eight of our pilots promoted to rank of general officer in the USMC. VMO-6 pilots promoted to this rank were: Lieutenant General E. Ehlert, Lieutenant General William R. Maloney, Lieutenant General William J. White, Major General Victor A. Armstrong, Brigadier General John C. Arick, Brigadier General Coleman D. Kuhn, Brigadier General Lloyd W. Smith, and Brigadier General Jerry E. Ward. Truly amazing!

★★★

The 13 months I was in Vietnam was probably the most valuable experience of my life; I was just a young man with little to no appreciation for being an American living in a free country with numerous opportunities ahead of me. Unfortunately, all of us did not make it back. Like everyone who was sent off to Vietnam the realities of war made us grow up in quick order. I can speak only for myself, but I believe that the rest of the aircrews in VMO-6 most likely had very similar experiences as I have written about in this book and have their own stories to tell. I believe I have matured into a better person because of our experience, and the missions that we all performed. For sure, I am fortunate enough to be sitting here writing these memoirs and hopefully giving proper credit to the pilots, the other crew chiefs, and the gunners in the squadron.

There are two events that most always jump out at me when thinking about my time in Vietnam. The first is early in my tour, the day that I was just an FNG gunner, and still very much green behind the ears, when Land Shark had sent us over to help that small convoy of Marines. The convoy had stopped just outside the small village with the black smoke rising from it. When we arrived just overhead of the Marines in those trucks, they started cheering and waving, giving us the thumbs up, and suddenly that young-kid mentality was still present in me in 1967. That was such an awesome, emotional feeling, and I knew that I had one of the best jobs in Vietnam.

The second incident was when we landed to pick up that poor little Vietnamese girl, whose only sin was being out in the nearby woods, with others in the village, just gathering firewood. She died in the hot sun right outside the civilian hospital while the medical staff there seemed to care less. Two very conflicting memories and emotions when I think back to Vietnam.

Whether or not we should have been there in Nam is not for me to say, and I certainly am not qualified to proffer an opinion. But I am convinced that the US military could not have won that war just sitting there in defensive positions. To all Marines who served in Vietnam and previous wars, and especially Marine Aviation, I am so proud to have been one of you.

Semper Fidelis!

Citations

MARINE OBSERVATION SQUADRON 6
Marine Aircraft Group 36
1st Marine Aircraft Wing
Fleet Marine Force Pacific
FPO, San Francisco 96602

7:GJH:gjh7B:aeb/39
1650   1650
2 December 1967

From: Commanding Officer
To: Corporal Peter N. GREENE 2213486 USMC

Subj: Award of 2 silver stars and 7 gold stars in lieu of the 8th through 16th Air Medals

Encl: (1) CG 1stMAW ltr 7B:aeb/39 1650 of 11Oct67
      (2) CG 1stMAW ltr 7B:twz/42 1650 of 20Oct67
      (3) CG 1stMAW ltr 7B:aeb/40 1650 of 11Oct67
      (4) CG 1stMAW ltr 7B:twz/6 1650 of 21Oct67

1. Delivered with pleasure.

W. J. WHITE

By direction

Copy to:
CMC (Code DGH) FOR FILE
SNCSLF w/2 copies of encl (1)
CG FMFPac

CITATIONS • 183

UNITED STATES MARINE CORPS
HEADQUARTERS 1ST MARINE AIRCRAFT WING
FLEET MARINE FORCE, PACIFIC

The President of the United States takes pleasure in presenting **two gold stars and a silver star in lieu of** a 20th, 21st and 22nd Air Medal to

CORPORAL PETER NOLAN GREENE
UNITED STATES MARINE CORPS

for service as set forth in the following

CITATION:

"For meritorious achievement in aerial flight as a designated **Crew Chief** with **Marine Observation Squadron 6** during combat support missions in support of the Republic of Vietnam against the insurgent communist guerilla forces (Viet Cong) from **25 October 1967** to **23 November 1967.** He contributed materially to the success of his squadron. His courage and devotion to duty in the face of hazardous flying conditions were in keeping with the highest traditions of the United States Naval Service."

FOR THE PRESIDENT

NORMAN J. ANDERSON
MAJOR GENERAL, U. S. MARINE CORPS
COMMANDING GENERAL
1ST MARINE AIRCRAFT WING

UNITED STATES MARINE CORPS
HEADQUARTERS 1ST MARINE AIRCRAFT WING
FLEET MARINE FORCE, PACIFIC

The President of the United States takes pleasure in presenting
a silver star in lieu of a 26th Air Medal to

CORPORAL PETER NOLAN GREENE

UNITED STATES MARINE CORPS

for service as set forth in the following

CITATION:

"For meritorious achievement in aerial flight as a designated **Crew Chief with Marine Observation Squadron 6** during combat support missions in support of the Republic of Vietnam against the insurgent communist guerilla forces (Viet Cong) from **19 December 1967** to **22 December 1967.** He contributed materially to the success of his squadron. His courage and devotion to duty in the face of hazardous flying conditions were in keeping with the highest traditions of the United States Naval Service."

FOR THE PRESIDENT

NORMAN J. ANDERSON
MAJOR GENERAL, U. S. MARINE CORPS
COMMANDING GENERAL
1ST MARINE AIRCRAFT WING

United States Marine Corps

Certificate of Appreciation

Presented to

Peter Greene

By the authority vested in me, it is my pleasure to express the grateful appreciation of our Nation and the United States Marine Corps. I want to acknowledge the support you and Kathy gave Mark and Pam over the past 30 years. Specifically, in 2007, during two wars, when you and Kathy moved to North Carolina to watch over your three young grand daughters while Mark and Pam deployed to Iraq and Afghanistan. Their service in the defense of our Nation would not have been possible without you. Please know that your sacrifice for our country is notable, and the Marine Corps thanks you. Your lifetime of actions exemplify our motto, Semper Fidelis!

Given under my hand this 31st day of May 2024.

D. A. OTTIGNON
LIEUTENANT GENERAL, U.S. MARINE CORPS
COMMANDING GENERAL
II MARINE EXPEDITIONARY FORCE